SOLVING "THE INDIAN PROBLEM"

SOLVING "THE INDIAN PROBLEM": THE WHITE MAN'S BURDENSOME BUSINESS

Edited by MURRAY L. WAX
and ROBERT W. BUCHANAN

A NEW YORK TIMES BOOK

New Viewpoints
A Division of Franklin Watts, Inc.
New York 1975

Library of Congress Cataloging in Publication Data

Wax, Murray Lionel, 1922-   comp.
    Solving "the Indian problem": the white man's
burdensome business.

    "A New York times book."
    Bibliography: p.
    1. Indians of North America—Government relations—
Addresses, essays, lectures.   I. Buchanan, Robert W.,
joint comp.   II. Title.
E93.W35   970.5   74-11312
ISBN 0-531-05364-4
ISBN 0-531-05567-1 (pbk.)

Dedicated to the memories of

CAPTAIN JACK (KEINTPOOS)
Modoc of valor, guardian of his people

FELIX S. COHEN
defender of justice and law between Indians and other Americans

ROBERT W. RIETZ
exemplar of friendship with understanding

TABLE OF CONTENTS

SOLVING "THE INDIAN PROBLEM":

I

INTRODUCTION

Labeling the native peoples of the Caribbean as "Indians" was a judicious error on the part of Columbus. In order to finance his expedition, he had had to persuade the Spanish Crown that sailing a reasonable distance westward he would reach "The Indies," that region of wealth and trade in Southeast Asia. The learned skeptics thought the sailing distance was considerably further, but Columbus won the favor of the Spanish Queen and she underwrote the voyage. Whatever land he encountered *had* to be the The Indies, and accordingly its inhabitants were to be referred to as "Indians" (*los Indios*).

Besides the geographical misrepresentation, the mislabel of "Indians" came to have further misleading consequences. The natives of the Americas had not identified themselves as a single people by whatever name. Rather, they had thought of themselves as members either of small bands of kith and kin or of somewhat larger tribal and linguistic units. In time, the diversity was recognized and names such as Apache, Pequot, Texocan, Natchez, Tlaxcaltec, and Eskimo entered the vocabulary of the Europeans and white Americans. Nevertheless, the misleading label of "Indian" did adhere and was stretched to fit all the natives of the Americas. Thus, by virtue of their relationship to the white invaders, the natives of the Americas found themselves classified under the single label of *Indian* (*Indio*), just as by virtue of capture and enslavement, the diverse natives of West Africa found themselves classified under the label of *Negro* (black).

The European invaders were a varied lot of many nationalities and professions. Some came to trade, some to loot, some to win souls for the Christian deity; and others came to settle land they thought of as vacant (or "wilderness") and to till it in the fashion of European peasants. With such differing goals, they had differing perspectives on the Indians and distinct notions of how these people were "a problem" and how that problem was to be resolved. Yet however different were their goals, they tended to classify the native Americans together and to indulge themselves with the notion that only temporarily would there be "an Indian problem." Temporary because the Indians were to be temporary. *Indian* problem because it was the Indians who were problems for the whites (even though it was the whites who were invading the Indians' lands and seizing their resources). And, *an* Indian problem, rather than problems of whites and Indians, because after all Indians were defined as alike in being heathens, savages, and non-Europeans.

Some whites thought that this Indian problem was most simply resolved through extermination, and that awful process did in fact occur repeatedly in the New World. The Spanish conquistadors enslaved the natives of the island of Santo Domingo and worked them to death; the miners seeking gold regarded the Indians of California as pestiferous vermin and massacred them. Against such horrors, missionaries insisted that the Indian was a being who possessed a divine soul, and they tried to protect him from the violence of their countrymen. To the missionaries the Indian was a benighted or savage man who required instruction in Christianity and the traits of civilized European society. While most missionaries thought of the Indian as capable (potentially) of being assimilated into European or white society, other observers and reformers thought in terms of a pluralistic division of the continent. To these observers it seemed as if large areas were so inhospitable and so lacking in resources as to be fit only for Indian habitation, and from their perspective, the solution to the Indian problem was to gather that people together and to remove them from the more desirable areas and to confine them, forcibly if necessary, in the valueless lands of "Indian Territory."

The various Indian groups, being themselves diverse, responded in a variety of ways to the presence, the catastrophes and opportunities of the white invaders. Some concentrated on trade; some defended themselves and their resources; some learned the skills of the invaders. Whatever the processes, the lives of the native peoples were altered and reorganized not once but numerous times. And many tribal units that now are thought to be the most traditionally Indian only came into existence as Indians were striving to cope with the problems of invasion and cultural interchange. This is most easily evident in the case of the Plains Indians, for these peoples did not emerge as such until the Spanish brought the horse to the New World and until that animal went wild and acclimated itself. In time, various Indian groups discovered a new and rich life by domesticating the horse and using it to win their living from the bison (buffalo) and from raiding; so, a new series of tribes emerged, known as Plains Indians: the Sioux, Comanche, Cheyenne, Osage and others. Equally striking is the case of the Iroquoian peoples, who, in order to take advantage of the trade with the English, organized themselves as the League of the Six Nations and embarked on a policy of expansion that made them a major political power during the colonial period of North American history. During the Revolutionary War and the subsequent military engagements, the League became divided, its peoples were defeated and betrayed, and their lands were seized or swindled. Yet within the twentieth century their menfolk have emerged as an elite among construction workers, laboring on the high steel of bridges, dams, and skyscrapers.

Over the centuries, then, some Indian peoples were exterminated; some assimilated, intermarried, and disappeared; many were relocated into other territories; yet, nonetheless, a large number of Indian peoples adapted, readapted, and even readapted again, remaining recognizably Indian. To the extent that Indians possessed resources that whites wanted, they were considered "an Indian problem." When they lost those resources and became impoverished and ecologically disoriented, but managed tenaciously to endure, they were also "a problem"—a moral problem to whites who had acquired or inherited that which once had been Indian.

Through the medium of news stories and interpretative essays selected from a century of *The New York Times*, we shall see how whites have interpreted their relationships to the various native Americans and how they attempted to solve or mitigate the "Indian problem." Throughout this history there were clear-sighted men who realized that "the problem" was not being created by Indians but by whites seeking their possessions; but the issue has been muddled, not only by naked or greedy interest, but also by complex questions of national ideology.

In the cases of the Modoc War and of the Termination program of the early Eisenhower Administration, greed and interest seem to predominate, so that the "Indian problem" was simply "white business." During the Modoc War, the whites were occupying lands that previously had been inhabited by the Modoc peoples; they were bewildered and defensive, wishing to be at peace and wishing to live as and where they had always, and unable to adjust to the force of circumstances. In the case of Termination, the driving forces were similar, in that such resources as the forests of the Klamaths and the Menominee were tempting to white interests, but the ideological questions had grown more complex.

In a sense the "Indian problem" has been the ideological and political problem of the United States. Given that ours is a nation composed of many peoples—a union of states and an amalgamation of ethnicities—how shall we live and be united together? Despite the multitude of languages of the native Americans and early settlers, our predominant language has become English; is it equally true that we must conform to a common Anglo culture? Must Indians continue to shed whatever remains of their original cultures and emerge as what Indian nationalists derisively label "apples" (namely, red on the outside, but Anglo white on the inside)? Alternatively, will the process be more equalitarian but just as homogenizing, namely a blending or assimilating together of these diverse stocks, as evident by the facts that both whites and Indians now eat maize (corn) and smoke tobacco (both domesticated by Indians), while most worship a deity whose creed emerged among Mediterranean peoples, and all live by a code of laws formalized on the basis of Anglo-Saxon tradition?

All along, there have been those who have rejected Anglo-conformity and assimilation and have contended that the United States must be pluralistic, so that the United States would continue to exist as a mixture of ethnic and religious groups who each would remain socially and culturally distinctive. The Indians as a kind of "charter minority" would then be the groups most entitled to maintain traits and privileges setting themselves apart from other Americans.

In the news stories and essays that follow these ideologies are represented, sometimes in pure form, sometimes in blends. The justification for the policy of Termination (as for the earlier policy of "Allotment") was what could be called "Anglo-conformity." Indians had to learn to live the way Anglos live. The way to achieve that goal was by a policy of "sink or swim"—throw the Indians on their own to fend as individuals for themselves in the same fashion as Anglos thought of themselves as rearing their own young. The Indian New Deal and the Community Action Programs of the War on Poverty had an opposed, often pluralistic, philosophy. Indians could remain identifiably Indian, but they were to be assisted and directed—encouraged or instructed—to adopt new and better patterns of conduct, which were to be brought to them by benevolent authorities such as federal agencies. Thus the pluralistic ideology is accompanied by an Anglo-conformist undertone that exhorts Indians that they had better stop drinking so much alcohol, that they had better take better care of their children, that they had better adopt new habits of sanitation, or that they had better begin the hard process of learning to support themselves without governmental subsidies and assistance. Such exhortations seem natural and even "liberal" until challenged by an Indian nationalist such as Vine Deloria, Jr., who blames Indian difficulties on the white invaders and despoilers and insists on the rights of Indian peoples to determine their own courses of living. To those who declare that this would be all right if Indians only supported themselves and demanded less of the government, he responds by noting that what is demanded is not charity but the fulfillment of contractual obligations embodied in treaties and legislation, and what Indians then do with their monies is their own business. He and other Indian nationalists (and cultural pluralists) also emphasize that Indians were and are capable of sustaining themselves providing that their lands, their water resources, and other properties are not seized, preempted, or otherwise swindled from them.

II

THE MODOC WAR:
Giving an Indian Tribe
"The Business"

Following the Civil War, an increasing number of settlers moved westward and so came into conflict with the Indians of the region. To reduce such conflict, President Ulysses S. Grant formulated what was called a "Peace Policy," predicated on a division of the West into areas reserved for Indians and those available to whites. Indians were instructed that they were free and secure while on their reservations, but that should they wander away from them, they would then be subjected to military retribution.

The intent of the Peace Policy was just that—to limit the number and violence of armed encounters between Indians and whites; but since the settlers were pushing into areas that were occupied by Indians, there were bound to be outbreaks. The circumstances and attitudes of both Indians and whites are revealed in the following series of news stories and articles documenting the Modoc War of 1872–73.

From the perspective of the whites, the antecedent of the war was the failure of a portion of the Modoc Tribe to abide by an 1864 treaty that had placed them on a reservation shared with the Klamath. However, the Modoc regarded the Klamath as enemies and wanted anyway to return to their traditional homes. Moreover, it is likely that they could not comprehend the land transfer entailed by the treaty. Under the leadership of

Keintpoos, known to whites as Captain Jack, a fairly sizable band left the reservation in the spring of 1870 and, together with other small bands, moved back to their home area near the Lost River in southern Oregon. Various attempts were made to induce the Modoc to return to the Klamath Reservation, and at least one governmental agent, being knowledgeable about their problems, suggested that a separate reservation be established for them. But no decision was reached until the fall of 1872 by which time the white population, now sizable, felt disquieted by the presence of the Modoc, whom they regarded as a nuisance if not a threat. The whites prodded the government into action, which came in the form of an order for the return of the Modoc to the Klamath Reservation. That order initiated a crisis in which the men of good will—Indians and whites—came to suffer, as described in the following stories.

The Modoc War | A speck of war scarcely "bigger than a man's hand," but yet threatening consequences of a serious character, appears in the accounts of the Modoc troubles which have reached us in the latest California papers. From these statements it appears that the Modoc Indians, who have long been troublesome to the settlers of Northern California and Southern Oregon, have finally resorted to open resistance to the military power of the United States, and have been guilty of those indiscriminate outrages upon settlers which experience has shown to be inseparable from all Indian outbreaks. Thus far we have news that a battle has been fought, in which the United States troops seem to have been worsted, for the Indians retired from the field to pillage the settlements and murder the white inhabitants in the vicinity of their camp at the mouth of Lost River.

It may be that we have, as yet, only a partial account of the origin of these troubles; but, from all the facts which have reached us, it appears that the Modocs have from the beginning been the aggressors. For several months past they have been sullen without cause, and, in consequence of the annoyances to which they subjected the settlers, an order was obtained from the Commissioner of Indian Affairs, requiring them to remove to the reservation. "Captain Jack" and "Scar-faced Charley," the Chiefs of the tribe, flatly refused to obey this order, and the Indian Super-

SOURCE: *New York Times*, December 22, 1872.

intendent of the district then called upon Major Jackson, the United States commander at Fort Klamath, to enforce it. This officer having two companies of troops available, started with thirty-five men to subdue over one hundred resolute savages, skilled in the use of those fire-arms with which they were fully supplied; and, as might have been expected, his command was worsted in the skirmish which ensued upon his arrival at the Indian camp. Up to this time, the Modocs had not committed any murders, but immediately after this fight they abandoned their camp, with the women and children, to the soldiers, and, starting out upon a foray, killed every white man they met. Not content with murder, they resorted to rapine, and pillaged and burned several settlements. Up to the date of our last mail advices, the Modocs had not been checked, and we are not surprised to learn from the latest accounts that there is danger of a general Indian uprising, and that intense excitement exists throughout the threatened region.

This story, in all its details, only repeats the incidents which have attended the advance of civilization across the Continent for nearly a century. The whites have, in the first instance, perhaps, been guilty of needless aggravations, but whether that has been the case or not, there have certainly been gross blunders in the coercive portion of the proceedings. When it was determined to remove the Modocs to the reservation, a force should have been employed large enough to have made resistance impossible, and the removal might have been effected without the firing of a gun or the loss of a life. In consequence of the policy which was adopted, the Indians were encouraged to defy the authority of the Government, many Modocs and whites have been slain, several ranches destroyed, a large area of country disturbed, and animosities engendered which will require many years to remove.

A general Indian rising in the Pacific States is a matter of serious consequence to the whole country, and all possible means should be used to avoid such a calamity. The Modoc War, as far as it has gone, does not appear to be a credit to anybody concerned; it may become a reproach to the entire nation. The Indian policy of President Grant, if properly carried out, would render such affairs impossible, and that it has not done so in this case has been plainly due to the errors of subordinate agents. We hope that these, if found equal to the duty, will be required to repair their mistakes, or that they will be replaced by others of more discretion and nerve.

> This "speck of war" received such great play in the newspapers of the day that the West Coast reports would lead the reader to believe that a major uprising was underway. The sharp fight and subsequent raids on white settlers (none of which seems to have been perpetrated by Captain Jack's immediate followers) caused such an uproar that the Modocs were forced to flee to the natural fortifications of the "lava beds" of northern California. Although the area of the lava beds was not coveted by white settlers, there was an intense desire, as illustrated in the following article, for the capture and confinement of these "savages" who would raid white settlements.

Capt. Jack and the Modocs | The success of the Modocs in their first encounters with our troops has made their chief, Capt. Jack, somewhat exacting in his conditions for a "big talk." When he sought an interview with Messrs. Dorris and Fairchild, he insisted that these gentlemen must come to his camp; a proper sense of his own dignity would not permit the chief to go to them. It is to be hoped that he will be more gracious when the Commissioners, recently appointed by the Indian Department, visit his country, as otherwise it may not be possible to carry out their pacific intentions. Yet, the individual who is thus punctilious about a meeting, is the leader of a band of not more than 400 savages, and his fighting force is even less than this. It is not, therefore, unlikely that it may become necessary to administer "dis-

SOURCE: *New York Times*, February 8, 1873.

cipline" to the Modocs before they can be brought to a sense of their true position and the power of the general Government. A place was provided for these Indians, some three years ago, on the Klamath Reservation; but Capt. Jack objected to live on the same reservation with his hereditary enemies, the Klamaths. So he and a band of warriors, some 300 in number, refused to be confined by its limits, and have roamed over the country whithersoever their savage will has led them, appropriating such property as they needed or desired, and scalping any white settlers who presumed to interfere with them. The restriction of their future wandering to the Oregon coast reservation, as is suggested by the Acting Commissioner of Indian Affairs, is a most desirable arrangement.

The plan of reservations for Indians is generally approved by army officers and in fact by all who are best acquainted with the habits of the red men, as being best united, for the protection of settlers in their vicinity, and as a means of introducing civilization among the savages. But to give any force to this policy, Indians found off their reservations must be punished, and the authorities of the tribes be held strictly responsible for any depredations committed by their warriors or young men. If the actual offenders cannot be specified, it must be made the business of the chiefs to find them out, and bring them to justice. This will naturally lead to the establishment of some sort of judicial system by the Indians; but they can readily achieve this, and it will be a decided advance with them toward civilized usages. As an offset to this, some tribunal must be appointed before which the Indian may bring any complaint he may have to make against a settler or an agent, for it is unfortunately the case that the redskins are not always the aggressors or the most guilty parties. The present Indian policy of the Government covers most of this ground, but it has not been the uniform custom to promptly punish such Indians as leave their reservations without authority, or insist upon bringing to justice every Indian who murders a white person. The savages have a clear enough comprehension of the reservation laws, but they have seen them so frequently broken with impunity that they are likely to cease to respect them entirely.

If Capt. Jack and his Modocs had been forced to return to the reservation assigned to them when they first left it some time ago, they would probably have remained there, and the present war in Oregon would have been avoided.

> While reports from the coast indicated that troops were on the way to "exterminate" the Modocs who had taken refuge in the lava beds, a military solution was not, at first, resorted to. Although the military build-up continued, a peace commission was appointed and dispatched to the area to attempt a negotiated settlement. The instructions to the commissioners were as follows:

Important Order from the Commissioner of Indian Affairs—A Humane Policy to Be Pursued | WASHINGTON, February 5—By direction of the Secretary of the Interior, Col. H. R. Clum, Acting Commissioner of Indian Affairs, to-day issued the following instructions to the commissioners recently appointed to investigate and remove the causes of the difficulties with the Modoc Indians. It will be seen that the temper of the instruction keeps most prominently in view the humane policy which has thus far been the distinguishing feature of Government dealing with the Indians:

Department of the Interior,
Office of Indian Affairs
Washington, D.C., Feb. 5.
Sir:

Having been appointed by the honorable Secretary of the Interior a Special Commissioner on behalf of this Department, to be associated with Jesse Applegate, Esq., of Yoncalla, Oregon, and Samuel Case, Esq., United States Indian Agent for the Alsea subagency in said State, for the purpose of

SOURCE: *New York Times*, February 6, 1873.

proceeding to the scene of the troubles with the Modoc Indians, in the State of Oregon, the following detailed instructions are given for your guidance. The commission, before entering upon the active discharge of its duties will confer with Gen. E. R. S. Canby, and for this purpose will arrange to meet him at the most available point. It is suggested that Linkville be selected as the place of meeting. The commission will also confer in subsequent proceedings with Gen. Canby, and will act under his advice as far as possible, and always with his co-operation. The objects to be attained by the commission are these: First—To ascertain the causes which have led to the difficulties and hostilities between the United States troops and the Modocs, and, second, to devise the most effective and judicious measures for preventing the continuance of these hostilities and for the restoration of peace. It is the opinion of this department, from the best information in its possession, that it is advisable to remove the Modoc Indians, with their consent, to some new reservation, and it is believed that the coast reservation in Oregon, lying between Cape Lookout on the north, and Cape Perpetua on the south, and bounded east by the coast range of mountains, and on the west by the Pacific Ocean, will be found to furnish the best location for these Indians. The commission will, therefore, endeavor to effect an amicable arrangement for locating these Indians on some portion of these reservation [sic] possible for it to do so, and provided that the commission is not of opinion, after fully investigating the case, that some other place is better adapted to accomplish the purpose of the department, in either of which events the commission will, before finally concluding an arrangement with the Indians, hold communication with the office and receive fuller advice. The commission will in nowise attempt to direct the military authorities in reference to their movements. It will be at liberty, however, to inform the commanding officer of the wish of the department, that no more force or violence be used than in his opinion shall be deemed absolutely necessary and proper, it being the desire of the department in this, as well as in all other cases of like character, to conduct its communications with Indians in such a manner as to secure peace and obtain their confidence, if possible, and their voluntary consent to a compliance with such regulations as may be deemed necessary for their present and future welfare. By the second article of the treaty concluded with the Klamath and Modoc tribes of Indians, Oct. 14, 1854, the following tract of country was set apart as reservations for said Indians, viz.: Beginning upon the eastern shore of Middle Klamath Lake, at a point of rocks about twelve miles below the mouth of Williamson River;

thence following up said eastern shore to the mouth of Wood River; thence at Wood River to a point one mile north of the bridge at Fort Klamath; thence due east to a summit of the ridge which divides the Upper and Middle Klamath Lakes; thence along said ridge to a point due east of the north end of the Upper Lake; thence due east, passing the said north end of the Upper Lake to the summit of mountains on the east side of the lake, thence along said mountains to a point where Sprague River is intersected by the Ish-tish-ea-wap Creek, thence in a southerly direction to the summit of the mountains, the extremity of which forms the point of rocks; thence along said mountain to the place of beginning; and it was stipulated by the same articles that the tribes aforesaid agree and bind themselves that immediately after the ratification of this treaty they will remove to said reservation and remain thereon, unless temporary leave of absence be granted them by the superintendent or agent having charge of the tribes. The Modocs, however, or that portion of them not now on the reservation, have refused to locate thereon on account of the Klamaths, with whom they are not on terms of amity. Instructions were given to Superintendent O. Deneal, under date of 12th of April last, to have the Modocs removed, if practicable, to the said reservation, and to protect them from the Klamaths; but that if they could not be removed or kept on the reservation, to select and report the boundaries of a new reserve for them. It is presumed that the attempt to permanently locate those Indians has had the effect to dissuade them in some degree; but of this fact the commission will be enabled to judge in the course of its investigations. The commission will keep the department advised as frequently as possible of its progress until the work which is assigned to it shall be accomplished, or its further progress proven to be unnecessary, when a final report will be submitted to this office.

Very respectfully, your obedient servant,

H. R. CLUM,
Acting Commissioner

A. B. MEACHAM, ESQ.,
Commission Chairman,

Washington, D.C.

The "humane policy" outlined in Washington underwent a severe test in the case of the Modocs. The Modocs themselves had specific demands—a separate reservation, preferably on

Lost River, and amnesty from state prosecution for the killing of the settlers—and so did the whites—that "the crimes of the Modocs not be condoned by the Commission" and that a plan for a new reservation on Lost River not be entertained.

Despite these obstacles, the commission, working closely with General Canby, commander of the army forces in the area, attempted to get negotiations underway with Captain Jack, whom they considered the leader of all the Modocs. As was often the case in Euro-American negotiations with native Americans, the peace commissioners expected Captain Jack to speak for and to rule his people as a body. Jack functioned, however, as a leader only so long as the people chose to follow him. As the negotiations progressed—slowly to be sure—Jack suggested settlement on terms other than those the Modocs had originally demanded. Several of the chiefs who had joined Jack's group for protection after the raids on white settlements called Jack "an old woman" and demanded that he take a more forceful line. With his manhood under question, Captain Jack was forced to commit an overt act to reaffirm his fitness for leadership and to place himself on the same level with the chiefs who had committed the murders. He was forced to pledge to kill General Canby to maintain his position.

Jack sought a meeting with the peace commissioners and General Canby and was accepted by them, as his request appeared a hopeful sign. After a brief discussion, Jack gave a signal and shot General Canby. In the shooting that followed, one peace commissioner was killed and another seriously wounded. Public reaction to the incident was immediate and intense—especially in the nearby area where cries for the total extermination of the Modoc band were the rule. The following article illustrates national reaction to the murders and is particularly revelatory of attitudes of whites toward Indians in the late nineteenth century.

The Modoc War. Feeling in Washington—Views of President Grant, Gen. Sherman, and Other Officials | WASHINGTON, April 14—The Modoc massacre has been the exclusive topic of consideration and discussion here to-day, and the inquiries for further particulars have been constant, but no official dispatches have been received to-day. Everywhere there has been manifested a vigorous approval of the orders which have been given by the President and Gen. Sherman for the severest punishment of these treacherous wretches, even to their extermination if necessary.

Views of the President

The President, in conversation to-day, said there would be no hesitation in dealing with this band as their crimes deserved, but at the same time orders for severity in their case were not to be interpreted as authority or license for war or outrage against the Cheyennes, Arrapahoes, Sioux, or other tribes, who are now all peaceably disposed. The country may rest assured that there will be no change in the President's policy toward the Indians; that he will continue to encourage the belief on their part that they will be well treated if they behave themselves, but at the same time will punish, as in this case, with unsparing severity, any conduct which defies the authority or injures the servants of the Government.

Gen. Sherman's Sentiments

A reporter who visited Gen. Sherman to-day, asked him if he did not believe this act of Indian treachery was unparalleled, upon which he replied in his quick, nervous way:

"No, Sir. Treachery is inherent in the Indian character. I know of a case where the Indians murdered the man who not two hours before had given them food and clothing."

The General then related several instances of Indian treachery and barbarity of which he became cognizant when in the West. He says the President is deeply affected by the death of Gen. Canby, and fully con-

SOURCE: *New York Times*, April 15, 1873.

curs with him in believing that no mercy whatever should be shown toward the Modocs. Gen. Sherman has perfect confidence in Gens. Schofield and Gillem, and believes they will be fully equal to the task of punishing the Modocs. He does not think the Modocs will be able to escape, although the topography of the lava beds is something of a puzzle to him.

Declaration of Secretary Delano

Secretary Delano declares that he will ask no mercy for the Modocs, as they have acted in the most outrageous and cowardly manner, and are therefore no longer entitled to any protection under any policy. He does not think this affair will permanently damage the so-called peace policy. It is not an object of the peace policy to deal with hostile Indians leniently. Its object is to protect Indians as long as they behave themselves, but when they become unruly and hostile, the Interior Department turns them over to the military. "There is Cochise," said the Secretary today, "he has gone on a reservation, and we will protect him there. But these thieving bands of Apaches now out will be dealt with by the military authorities."

In response to a remark that the peace policy did not seem to be understood, the Secretary said:

"Yes, that is the case. But I think this terrible affair will serve to bring about a better understanding of it. There were circumstances about this thing which can never occur again. A traditional feud between the Klamaths and Modocs was one of these circumstances, and again there were a lot of half breeds among these Modocs who persuaded them not to give up, and represented to them that they would be hung or otherwise severely punished. A lot of bad white men among them also kept up the feeling for war as they wanted to sell their corn."

Mr. Delano further said that Gen. Canby had been in perfect accord with his department, and he had every confidence in him. He had full power in the premises. He could remove a commissioner if necessary, and do just as he pleased.

"The Indians have murdered their best friend," exclaimed Mr. Delano. "I hope they will be punished severely, and shall ask for no mercy for them."

What Commissioner Smith Says

Commissioner Smith took the same view as the Secretary of the Interior upon the effect which this event would have upon the peace policy. He said that the peace policy does not mean that Indians are to maraud and murder as they please, but only that friendly Indians shall be governed by it. Hostile Indians are to be ruled by the army when necessary, and the instructions to Mr. Meacham will show this. Of Gen. Canby, Mr. Smith said that he was an excellent officer, and the last man that we could afford to spare, the General having been selected for the position out there on account of his coolness, his good judgment, his desire to do justice to the Indians, and his entire accord with the department.

"The peace policy has sustained its greatest loss by the death of Gen. Canby," remarked the commissioner. "He was just the officer we needed at points where delicate matters were to be settled between the settlers and Indians. I believe if this peace policy had been commenced eight years ago and carried out faithfully until this time we would have no trouble now with the Indians. The death of Gen. Canby cannot be called a defeat of the peace policy, as the Modoc business was as much of a military movement as a peace movement. It was a movement well planned and well carried out by an able officer."

Topography of the Lava Beds

Dr. Stevenson, of Prof. Hayden's Geological Survey, who explored these lava beds two years ago, is of the opinion that the troops will find it a work of great difficulty to dislodge the bloodthirsty Modocs from their secure retreat. This region, between Tule Lake and Clear Lake, and for many miles south and north, is of a very extraordinary formation. The igneous and basaltic rock has been thrown up in immense piles by volcanic action, and the lava is from 10 to 30 feet thick, interspersed with numerous fissures, which connect with the caves and holes in the rocks, which are very extensive, intersecting each other, and some of them large enough to encamp a company of men. Streams flow through these caverns and disappear outside under the beds of lava. They also abound in animal life, such as rabbits, mice, and lizards, and a small party of Indians could subsist in them for a considerable time. The Indians understand these subterranean communications thoroughly, and it will doubtless be some days before any progress is made toward penetrating their retreat successfully.

> Certainly no "leniency" toward the Modocs was planned on the front. The troops were successful in driving Captain Jack's small band from the lava beds amid enthusiastic reports from the front. A *Times* entry of April 17, 1873 reports, "The troops are in excellent spirits and anxious to pursue the Modocs. Part of them [the soldiers] occupy the Lava Beds now and will prevent any Modocs from returning. Everything is working admirably, and we hope to chronicle the death of the last Modoc within a week. Too much praise cannot be awarded the officers and men."
>
> Jack was not, however, so easily caught. Only when some of the very subchiefs who had forced Jack to kill Canby betrayed him in exchange for amnesty and served as scouts for the army were they successful in forcing Jack and his band to surrender. The last article is an account of Captain Jack's trial for the murder of General Canby and includes Jack's personal statement of defense—given while his gallows were being constructed outside the courtroom.

The Modoc Trials | FORT KLAMATH, Oreg., Wednesday, July 9, 1873—The Modoc trials were finished today, and have proved to be a very brief affair compared to the expecta-

SOURCE: *New York Times*, July 23, 1873.

tions generally had in advance. The court met for active business on Saturday, July 5, with Gen. Elliott as President and Major Curtis as Judge Advocate. Dr. Belden, of San Francisco, was present as a shorthand reporter, and the trial proceeded with great celerity.

The prisoners were on trial for the murder of Gen. Canby and Dr. Thomas, and the attempted assassination of A. B. Meacham, who was horribly wounded, and Leroy S. Dyar, who escaped, as their evidence will show. They were all in chains, and came in slowly, marshaled by the guard, with their irons clanking and their features lighted up with an uneasy expression of excited interest. The court-room improvised for the occasion was a barrack mess-room, not by any means a dignified apartment for the temple of justice, but a rather common one well whitewashed, but finished up within with rough boards. In the center were the members of the court sitting around a long table, on which, instead of law books, were laid the swords of the officers. The members of the court, besides those named, were captains Mendenhall, Pollick, Hasbrouck, and Lieutenant Kingsbury. On the left sat the prisoners on a long bench—Jack, Schonches John, Boston, Black Jim, and two inferior wretches named Broncho and Slollux, who came up with the guns and took a part. It must be borne in mind that every one of the four renegade Modocs—Hooker Jim, Bogus Charley, Steam-boat Frank, and Shack Nasty—were also at the massacre, but they have earned exemption by their treason to Captain Jack, and faithful service in insuring his capture.

Back of the Judge Advocate sat the interpreters, Frank Riddle and Tobe (his wife). Tobe was neatly dressed, and comprehended well the questions and answers. She is the own cousin of Captain Jack, and she owes it to his interference that she has several times escaped harm from the tribe.

At either end of the room soldiers sat with guns and bayonets in hand guarding the prisoners; spectators were also at either end, and occasionally during the trial there came ladies in as lookers-on. The court meant business, and Major Curtis, the Judge Advocate, proved to be efficient in that position.

Frank Riddle and Mr. Dyar were the first witnesses examined.

Mr. Meacham arrived the next day (Sunday), and took the stand on Monday, and gave in his statement a full and complete summary of the events just preceding and at the massacre. Also the expressions uttered by Gen. Canby and Dr. Thomas before going, and the friendly speeches they made at the time of the actual meeting with the Modocs when they were assassinated. This makes a mass of matter of so much value that I give it in full, so far as it would possess any interest for the public.

Evidence of Mr. Meacham

After giving an account of the earlier negotiations with the savages, Mr. Meacham told the story of the massacre as follows:

When we arrived at the council tent Boston and Bogus had already arrived, making seven Indians who were visible. They were all smoking except Dr. Thomas, who never smoked. They were smoking cigars which Gen. Canby had carried out.

There had been a little fire built fifteen or twenty feet off the council tent, and on the side directly opposite from our camp—a sage-brush fire. Gen. Canby and Dr. Thomas were standing nearer to the tent than the Indians were, around the little fire which had nearly burned out. There were stones in a natural circle, or they had been placed there around the fire, making a kind of half circle. Before dismounting from my horse I had taken my overcoat off, laying it on the horn of the saddle in front of me. When I dismounted I hung it on the horn of the saddle and dropped the rope of my horse on the ground, not tying him—reining him up with the bridle rein over the coat.

Mr. Dyar rode on the east side of the fire before dismounting—also Mrs. Riddle. When we got ready to talk we sat down around the fire, Gen. Canby facing Schonches John—these two being nearest the tent. Captain Jack sat next to Schonches John, and there were other Indians next to Capt. Jack, but I cannot now say who.

I can only define positively the positions of Schonches John and Capt. Jack; that I sat next to Gen. Canby, on his left; that Dr. Thomas sat on the ground—not on a stone—a little behind, and to my left. Mrs. Riddle sat or reclined on the ground near to Dr. Thomas, a little in front of him. Mr. Riddle was, a portion of the time, between Dr. Thomas and Mrs. Riddle; but after we had been talking a few minutes some of the Indians saw a man approaching from the camp, and at my request, Mr. Dyar mounted his horse and rode out to the man and sent him back. On Mr. Dyar's return to the council he dismounted from his horse on the side of the fire occupied by the Indians, to the right of Gen. Canby, and a little behind my horse. We had been talking perhaps fifteen minutes when Hooker Jim went to my horse, calling him by name, and tied the rope either to a rock or a little sage-brush grub, went to the saddle, took off my overcoat, buttoned it up from bottom to top, and said that he was Meacham, or that he would be Meacham. He turned to Bogus Charley and asked if he didn't look like old man Meacham. He said he was or would be, but I cannot say which way he said it; one way or the other, that he was or would be Meacham. I am not very positive whether he said, "I am Meacham now" or "I will be Meacham," but one or the other. I know that he asked Bogus Charley if he looked like "Old Meacham" (as I think the Modocs called me). He said it in English. That act was, in my judgment, a declaratory one, and sufficient evidence of what was coming. I sought to get a glance at Gen. Canby's face, and I am very confident, although no words were passed, that Gen. Canby understood the act, or knew what it meant. I think we talked fifteen or twenty minutes after that before any other demonstrations were made of a hostile nature. Dr. Thomas had made a very religious and conciliatory speech to the Indians, Gen. Canby a very friendly one, and Jack had finished talking. Said he talked all he wanted to. Schonches John was making a speech, which Riddle was interpreting. After Schonches John had finished his speech, or made a statement or declaration, and while Riddle was interpreting it, off on our left, and pretty near in range with the way we were sitting, two men that I did not recognize jumped up from ambush with one or more guns under each arm.

Question—Mr. Meacham, can you not tell the commission what Gen. Canby said to the Indians? Answer—Yes; I have a pretty good recollection of it. The substance I know exactly. After the demonstration of

Hooker Jim—the taking of the coat—fully appreciating the peril we were in, I asked Gen. Canby if he had any remarks to make—partly for an opportunity to look him in the face, and partly to see whether he could say something to avert the peril. Gen. Canby rose to his feet to talk, and said in substance: When he was a very young officer in the army, he was detailed to remove two different tribes of Indians—one from Florida, and one from some other part of the Southeast, to west of the Mississippi River. That at first they had not liked him very well—but after they got acquainted with him, they liked him so well that they elected him a chief among them. He then gave the name that each tribe had given him—one designating him a tall man or chief, the other the "Indians' friend," giving the Indian words; that years after they were located in their new home, he visited these people and found them prosperous and happy; that they came a long way to shake hands with him as a friend and brother; that he had no idea but that the Modocs would sometime recognize him as a friend when they were located in a home; that his life, or a greater portion of it, had been spent in the United States Army in the Indian service; that he had never deceived them; had always dealt fairly with them; that he came here by request of the President of the United States; that the President had ordered the troops here, and that they could only be removed by the President's order; that they were only here for the purpose of seeing that the commission did their duty and performed what they agreed to do; that these people (addressing them) should do what they agreed to do, and that the citizens should not interfere; that unless the President ordered it, he, Gen. Canby, could not take the soldiers away. This is about a synopsis of the General's speech. After Gen. Canby had spoken I turned again to Dr. Thomas, who was a little behind me, and the Doctor, in raising forward, came upon his knees and laid his right hand on my left shoulder, bringing him nearly even with me in this position—on his knees with his hand on my shoulder, he was so close to me. He said: "Tobe, tell these people that I think the Great Spirit put it into the heart of the President to send us here. I have known Gen. Canby for ten years, Mr. Dyar for a few years, and Mr. Meacham for eighteen years. I know their hearts and my own heart, and I believe God sees all that we do; that He wishes us all to be at peace; that no more blood should be shed." That is the substance. There were other little things, but they were immaterial. The substance of Jack's speech was that he wanted the soldiers taken away. That was the main point. Schonches John's speech was that he wanted Fairchild's Ranch or Hot Creek. These were the main points. The reply was that the President had sent the soldiers there—that they could not be taken away without his consent. I think I said that myself, and that Gen. Canby repeated it—that they were sent there by the President, and could not be removed without his consent. Schonches John said he was willing to accept of Hot Creek for a home; that he had been informed that he could have that place. He was asked, "Who told you you could have it? Did Fairchild or Dorris?" He replied that they did not. "But from what other source did you learn you could have that place?" Then Schonches John said: "Unless the soldiers are taken away, and you give us Hot Creek or Fairchild's Ranch, we don't want to talk any more."

The interpreter had rendered that speech of Schonches John pretty nearly, perhaps not quite finished it, when the two men sprang up. When the men came in sight, we all rose to our feet except Mr. Riddle, who I think threw himself flat on the ground. While Schonches John was talking, Capt. Jack had risen, and turning his back, was walking off a few steps, perhaps behind Mr. Dyar's horse or toward it. He was coming again toward the circle at the time the Indians rose up. He was rather facing it. But when the Indians made their appearance, I asked the question of Capt. Jack: "What does that mean?" He made no reply to me directly. He put his right hand under the left breast pocket and drew his pistol, and sung out some words in Indian which I did not then understand. I became satisfied they were all armed some time before that. I saw the two men who appeared from the rocks come up right before the first pistol was fired. Capt. Jack and Schonches John changed places, bringing Capt. Jack in front of Gen. Canby, and Schonches John in front of me. Capt. Jack drew his pistol and the cap busted, but did not discharge. He aimed it at Gen. Canby, and within less than three feet, pointed toward Gen. Canby's head. There had been no angry words, no act of any kind that would have provoked hostilities, that I know of. On the contrary, we were sedulously careful to avoid it, and I believe we all appreciated the necessity of being careful in conversation and in action. But after the assault of Capt. Jack with the pistol on Gen. Canby, what I remember most distinctly was that Schonches John drew his pistol from his left side, within not to exceed 3 or 4 feet from me. He discharged it at me, aiming evidently at my head. After drawing the pistol, almost the same time or very nearly, he drew a knife which he held in his left hand. He did not hit me at that time. He subsequently did shoot me. The ball, which struck me in my face [showing], was discharged from the pistol in the hands of Schonches John within 15 or 16 feet of me, after I had taken the cover of a rock. There was more firing, and the firing was very hot, and they were all very active making hostile demonstrations on the Peace Commission party. One man was after Dyar, I know, but I cannot tell who. I saw Dyar running and Riddle running, and I saw some man chasing him, but I cannot designate the man who did it, only they were of the party who were in the council.

Question—Did you still retain your senses after the ball had struck you in the forehead? Answer—A very short time afterward. Very soon I received a shot in my wrist, and a few moments after lost my consciousness, probably from the grazing shot on my temple. I remained unconscious until the skirmish line of rescuers came up. I received a shot in my left hand, my right wrist, my face, the end of my ear, and side of my head, and a knife-cut 4 or 5 inches in length on the side of my head, besides bruises. As soon as Jack fired the party of Indians sprang up and commenced firing, and all drew arms and were engaged in it some way. I did not see Gen. Canby after Capt. Jack had cocked his pistol to shoot the second time. I saw Dr. Thomas after he received his first shot, and my memory is that Boston was shooting at him. Dr. Thomas got on his right hand without falling entirely to the ground. I fell back about thirty or forty steps after the firing began; succeeded in running that distance. I recovered my senses when the skirmish line of Col. Miller's command came up. I suppose it must have been the time it required to march from headquarters on the double-quick. I came to consciousness when the line came up, hearing the voice of Col. Miller straightening his line; that is the first sound I remember.

During the trial the prisoners took great interest in the proceedings, at least some of them did. Broncho and Slollux were of a stupid order of even Indian nature, and evidently did not comprehend much. One of them drew his knees up to his chin and sat with his hat on and his head down, Capt. Jack sat with intelligent look, and actively watching the course of the trial, Schonches John was intensely interested, but did not seem to understand himself or the occasion to advantage. Jack smoked his pipe occasionally and would lie over loungingly on the shoulder of Boston, (who sat next to him.) Boston is young looking and wears a very deceitful face and uncertain eye. The remaining prisoner was Black Jim, an intelligent-looking fellow, whose record of rascality, falsehood, treachery, and depravity has long been full.

As the evidence was taken down it was occasionally read over to the interpreter, and by him translated to the prisoners in full, and at the end of each witness' testimony the Modocs were asked if they wished to put any questions, but they always declined.

After the prosecution closed, Jack was asked to say what he wanted, and he desired to call for several persons—Scar-face Charley, Dave, and One-eyed Mose. These all testified as to the charges made against the Klamaths that they had furnished the Modocs ammunition at the battle of Jan. 17 in the lava beds, and promised them not to shoot at them. There were a number of Klamaths in that battle employed as scouts. In the late talk with Allen David, the Klamath head chief, Jack was decidedly discomfited, and he took this time to have his say about the Klamaths, a matter entirely irrelevant to the trial; but the Judge Advocate let the men say their say, probably as a concession to the pride and ignorance of the Modoc Chief.

It was expected that Capt. Jack would be on hand with a speech, for when asked to cross-question the witnesses he had said that he had no questions to ask, but wished to talk himself after a time, and was assured by the court that he could have the opportunity.

On Tuesday his witnesses were on the stand, and Schonches John spoke for a while, but to no purpose. Jack asked as a favor that when he spoke the renegade scouts might be present to hear him, and when the court met after noon they were all there.

Capt. Jack's Speech

Intimating that he would speak of the white men who were his friends, Capt. Jack said:

Judge Rosborough always told me, "Be a good man; I know the white man's heart, but not the Indian's heart as well." He never gave me any but good advice. "I have known a great many white people; have known that a great many of them had good hearts. I do not know all the Indian chiefs around; I do not know what their hearts are." Rosborough always told me to be a good man. I considered myself like a white man, and didn't want an Indian heart any longer. I took papers (certificates of character) from good white people, who gave me good advice. I know all the people around me, and they all know I was an honest man. People around Yreka all knew me; knew I acted right and did nothing wrong. You men here don't know what I have been before. I never called any white man mean. When I went to any that knew me and asked for a good paper they gave it, telling people who went through my country that I was a good Indian and never disturbed anybody. No white man can say I told him not to come to my country. I told them to come and gave them a home there. I should like to see the man who would accuse me of doing wrong. I have always been honest with every man. The Klamaths were the only people who said my papers were bad. I have never known any other Indian Chief who has spoken so much in favor of white men as I have. I have always taken their part, and spoken in their favor. I have done as my friends advised me, and have looked after white people who have traveled through my country.

I would like to see the man who came to Lost River last Winter and commenced this trouble, and so got me into this condition I am now. I cannot see why they got mad at me. I always told white people to come and live there, for that the country was their's as much as it was Capt. Jack's.

I have never received anything except what I bought and paid for. I have always lived like a white man. I have lived peaceably on what I could kill with my gun, and catch with my traps. You [to the interpreter] know that I have lived like a man, and never begged, got what I could honestly, with my own hands. I always took your good advice until this war started. I don't know how to talk here. Don't know how white people talk. Shall do the best I can.

I have never asked white people for pay to live in my country. I wanted them to come. I liked to live with white people—told them to live there and we would all be peaceable. I knew nothing of when this war was to commence. Major Jackson came and commenced on us while I was in bed. When Meacham used to come, he was always friendly, and never talked about shooting. I understood Ivan Applegate that he was coming to have a talk, and not that he was coming to bring soldiers. I was willing to hold councils with anyone who talked peace to me. The way I wanted that council to be. I wanted to have Henry Miller there when Applegate met me, and to have him talk for me. Dennis Crawley also told me he wanted to be there to talk with me when Applegate came. I was a good man, he said, and he wanted to have me get my rights.

It scared me when Jackson and his troopers came riding into my village at daylight. It made me get out of bed without even a shirt on. I couldn't imagine what it meant to have soldiers come that time of day. Major Jackson surrounded my camp, and then said for us not to shoot, for he wanted to talk. I told Bogus to go out and talk to them until I got my clothes on. Bogus didn't want to; but he went and told them that I wanted to talk, and not to shoot. Then they all got off their horses. I thought we were to have a talk, and went into another house to meet them. I thought then, Why are they mad at me? What have they found out about me that they have come here to fight me? I went into my tent and sat down, and then the soldiers commenced shooting. There were only a few of my people there. All were not there.

Major Jackson shot my men while they were standing around. I ran away and did not fight any. I did not want to fight. I took my people away who had been shot and wounded. They shot some of my women and some of my men. I didn't know anything about it.

After that I went off to the lava beds and did nothing. I had but very few people, and did not want to fight. Never did want to fight. Thought it was no use with so few. I went to the lava beds, and while on the way to my rock house (cave) a white man came to my camp. I told them how the soldiers had fought me while I was asleep, but that I would not do any harm to him.

After that I stayed in the lava beds and went nowhere at all. I did not want to fight, and did not think about fighting any man. I did not see any white man for a long time, and did not wish to kill anybody. I stayed there quietly in my cave.

After a while John Fairchild came and asked me if I wanted to fight. I told him, No; that I had quit fighting; that I did not want to fight any man; that I did not wish to fight him or to fight anybody; that I had quit and did not want to fight any more.

The Hot Creek Modocs did not come to the lava beds. They were not in the first fight on Lost River, and they concluded not to fight and to go on the reservation at Klamath Lake. When they got to Whittle's house, on Klamath River, the Linkville people came there to kill them. They came back to their old place. After that the Hot Creeks came to my camp and told me the white people were going to kill them all. The Hot Creeks all ran back and came to me. They were scared, as white men told them that they were going to kill them all. Some of the Hot Creeks were still left at Fairchild's, and they talked of taking them to the reserve by way of Lost River, and they ran off too and came to me. When they all got to my place I told some of them to go back to Fairchild's. The Hot Creeks came from one side to my place and Hooker Jim came around the other side of Tule Lake to get to the lava beds.

I didn't know of any settlers being killed until Hooker came there with his band and told me about it. I had no idea they would kill the Bostons [Yankees] when they went around that way. When they came, I didn't want them to go away. I don't know who told them to kill the settlers. I always told them not to kill white people. I told Hooker I had never killed any Bostons, and that he had done it of his own accord, and not by my advice. I thought all the white men in my country liked me, they always treated me so well.

[Turning to Hooker Jim, who was there by his special request, as were all the four renegades]—What did you kill them for? I did not want you to kill my friends; you did it on your own responsibility.

After that I thought all the Bostons would be mad at me. It troubled me and made me feel bad. I didn't want any of my people to kill the whites. I never advised them to do it. I told Hooker and his men it was a wicked act, and they ought not to have done it. I knew all the Bostons would be mad at me on account of Hooker's killing so many of their people when he had no business to do it.

I had not fought in the battle on Lost River, and I did not intend to fight anywhere. Fairchild told me what a wrong thing it was that they had killed these people living on Tule Lake, and that if we did not quit fighting, the soldiers would come and kill us all. I told him I did not want to fight, and was willing to quit if the soldiers would quit. I told him I was afraid to come to his house. He did not come for a long while after that. The Hot Creeks, some of them, came with him then. They left him soon after that, and he did not come for a long time. He was afraid to come any more.

For awhile I heard nothing from Fairchild. No one came to my place, and I could hear no news. After a great while Fairchild came again with a squaw, and said we had all better make peace, for the white people were all very mad at us.

For awhile there was nothing going on, and then the soldiers came again. They came fighting; fought all one day; they fought a little the first day, and then they fought all the next day. Then they went away again. Before the battle One-eyed Link River John came and told me not to be mad at them (the Klamaths), for they would not shoot at us. Some of the Klamath scouts came and had a talk with me then in the lava beds.

After that battle (Jan. 17) for a long time there was no fighting, nor was there any talking going on for a long while. Then Fairchild came again and said he wanted to have me come out and have a good talk. He said he and his people were mad at us for killing those citizens on Tule Lake. I told him I had never killed anybody, and never wanted to kill anybody, and didn't want any more war. I did not know what they were mad at me about, for I was willing for both sides to quit and live in peace again. I told him I did not now want the Lost River country any more, because there had been a war about it and bloodshed there, and that I wanted to go somewhere else; that I would like to go to some place where no blood had been shed as there had been there.

I don't deny that I told Fairchild and everybody else that I wanted to talk good talk and quit fighting. That was what I meant and what I told him.

My people were afraid to leave the caves because they had been told they would all be killed. My women were all afraid to go away from there. While the peace talk was going on a squaw came from Dorris' and Fairchild's, and said the Peace Commissioners wanted to get them out and kill them all; that a man named Nate Beswick had told them so. An old Indian man who was lately killed in a wagon on Tule Lake came over in the night to the lava beds and told the same story again. This old Modoc told me that Nate Beswick told him that that day Meacham, Canby, Dyar, and Thomas were going to get them out and kill them. Then another squaw came and told us the Peace Commissioners had a great lot of wood all piled up high, and intended to burn Jack on that pile of wood; that when they brought him to Dorris'—if ever they got him there—they would surely burn him alive. [That was at the time when tents were made ready for them at Dorris', and wagons sent for them, and they failed to come as agreed.] All the squaws about Dorris' and Fairchild's told the same thing. After hearing all this news I was afraid to go, and that is the reason I did not go and make peace.

[To Riddle, the interpreter]—You and your woman always told me the truth and advised me well, but I didn't take your advice. If I had listened to you instead of those squaws who were lying to me so, I would not be in all the trouble I am in now.

The reason I did not go when the wagons came after me was that squaws came the night before and told me the peace talkers were ready to burn me, and I was afraid to come. I can see now that those squaws and

Bob Whittles' woman lied to me. I would have been better off to have listened to you. Bob Whittles' woman came to me and said I was not one of her people, and she didn't wish to talk any thing good to me. She always gave me bad counsel. Bob's woman told me that if she did not come back right away we might know the soldiers would be coming the next day to fight me.

I have now told you all about why I did not come in and make peace. I was afraid to come. I don't consider that when you came to talk to me with the newspaper men that I was really the chief then. Your chiefs among the Bostons listen to the people, and the people listen to them and obey them, but my men would not listen. I told them not to fight, but they wanted to fight, and would not listen. I wanted to talk and make peace, and live aright, but my men would not listen. The Modoc men in the rock caves would not listen to what I said. There cannot one of them speak to me, and tell the truth, and say that I ever wanted them to fight. I always told them to keep out of trouble, and to meet in council in a friendly way. When they would not listen to me I told them if they wanted to fight it would have to be done, but not by my counsel.

As I was the chief of the Modocs, the Bostons probably all think I began the fight, and have kept it going. I have told the Modocs the white people would think so, and if they would surely fight they must do it on their own hook. Hooker Jim wanted to fight all of the time. I sat on one side all this while, with my few men who agreed with me, and said nothing. Now I have to bear the blame for what the rest of them have done. Schonches John was on Hooker's side. I was with a few men and had nothing to say, and they were all mad at me. I can't see how the Bostons think I am to blame for the war when it was those others who did the murders.

I talked to my people. I said, I like my wife and children, and I wish to live in peace and be happy with them. They would not stop to listen to me. I had nothing, had shot nobody, and did not commence the fight. Hooker always wanted to fight the Bostons, and it was he who did the murders. When I talked as I have said, Hooker and his friends told me to hush; that I knew nothing; that I was no better than an old squaw.

I and Hooker had a quarrel. I said I had done nothing wicked or mean to bring on the war; that it was he who had murdered the settlers. I got mad at Hooker, and if I could have seen through the wall of my tent, I would have killed him. I thought I would kill him. I wanted to kill him because he had murdered the settlers on Tule Lake, and had made the war worse.

When the fight commenced, I thought the Bostons were mad, because I wanted to live on Lost River. I had a fuss with an Indian named George, who took the part of Hooker Jim. We quarreled, and he told me I was no better than a squaw; that I had never killed anybody; that he and Hooker were not afraid, and had killed white people and lots of soldiers. He said: "You have never done any fighting, and you are our chief yet; you are not fit to be a chief."

I told him I wasn't ashamed of it; that I did not want to kill anybody. They told me that I laid in camp like a chunk, doing nothing, while they went around killing white people and stealing their things. They said they were Indians, and were not afraid to kill men. "What do you want of a gun? You do nothing with it. You don't kill anything, but sit around on the rocks."

I told them I was not ashamed to be called an old squaw; I had advised them to keep peace and kill nobody, and they had done these murders against my will.

Scar-face told me he could go and fight with the Modoc warriors, and that I was no better than an old squaw. I told them to go out and fight on their own account; I neither wanted to go with them or to live with them. Scar-face will tell what he knows. He does not want to keep anything back; neither do I wish to keep back anything.

Jack asked the privilege to add to his remarks the next morning, and the court indulged him in it. His words were few. He made a brief speech, reiterating some of his words of the day before, and insisting that Hooker Jim urged on the murder of the Peace Commissioners, and went out that day for the especial purpose to kill Meacham. This speech was made part of the records of the court, and ended the open sessions of the commission.

The decision of the court is not made public, but will be forwarded to

Gen. Davis for his approval, and be by him forwarded to Washington for review and approval by the President. Gen. Davis is several hundred miles distant in the Indian country, far away from mails and telegraphs, and cannot be reached and heard from in less than two or three weeks. The journey to Washington will occupy the remainder of the Summer, and the final disposition of Capt. Jack and his associates will be a case of *quien sabe* that may as well go undiscussed just at present. When red tape enough has been used up to do it with, some of them may be hung.

The trial of the Lost River murderers being turned over to the Oregon courts, we may expect them to be pretty thoroughly disposed of, and I doubt if they could ever receive justice in any other way save by the good offices of an Oregon jury. Capt. Jack's speech is considered by the court as rather dull and wanting in point, but it struck me that he made a very fair effort. The gentlemen of the court are not experts in Modoc oratory, and were evidently anticipating too much.

Capt. Jack showed far more understanding and intelligence than any other Indian on trial, and it is evident that his power all comes from the possession of more than average intellect and force of mind. As to the verity of his assertions, it must be remembered that he has been "a liar from the beginning," and that he was now endeavoring to make the very best of a very bad case. He rather humbled himself in some respects; abased himself to prevent his being too highly exalted on the gallows.

I am afraid that the purely and exclusively philanthropic people of the East who indulge in Indian worship and have little room for other sympathies, of which there seem to be a few, will find some texts for their peculiar emotions in Jack's speech; but it is to be hoped that they will remember that he is a terrible liar, and that upon a less than flimsy pretext he went out and took a leading part in the tragedy of April 11.

His speech to the court shows Captain Jack to have played much the role of the traditional Indian figure whom whites thought of as "chief." In small tribal societies, such as the Modoc, no man had the power to give orders to another. Whatever authority a man acquired was the consequence of age and wisdom; it was moral or spiritual, rather than coercive. A man was granted that kind of authority as he showed himself to be concerned with the welfare of all and to seek peace rather than conflict. The most severe task of a chief was to cope with young hotheads, the vigorous and proud men who wanted to take immediate and offensive action. When the chief was sustained by the consensus of the adults of the tribe, he might hope to control these warriors or moderate their conduct; but when many of the other adults were fearful and restive, and undercut his strivings for peace, the chief who continued to seek peace was open to the taunts of being a coward or old woman. To sustain his position, he might then be driven—as was Captain Jack—to an act of bravery, violence, and danger—an act that placed himself in the same or greater jeopardy than his associates with the ironical consequence that he was obliged to suffer (he was hanged) for their sins.

Implicit in these newspaper accounts are several tragedies. On the starkest level, there is the tragedy of the Modoc, who were hospitable to the white invaders and were then pushed from their hereditary lands onto a reservation with an ancient foe. Fleeing from this enforced intimacy, they became embroiled with hostile settlers and militia, and were caught within a series of reciprocal raids and massacres. Overwhelmed by panic and the rumors of white revenge, they pressured their leaders, who struck desperately at the nearest available targets—the most concerned and decent among the white population. To the Yankee troopers, the flag of truce established a sacred ground that must be respected even by the most bitter of enemies. When the Modoc violated that ground, the soldiers were confirmed in their belief that these were creatures beyond the pale of moral conduct. Yet the speeches by Meachem and Jack disclose that each was a man willing to risk his life for the sake of principle and manly honor. At another time and in other circumstances, Meachem, Canby, and Jack might have saluted each other as peers and comrades.

III

THE NEW DEAL:
Getting Indians
into the Business

With the Wheeler-Howard Act (or Indian Reorganization Act)
of 1934, the United States government committed itself to a
policy favoring self-determination and self-government, as
well as education and social services, for the native Americans.
The Meriam Report of 1928 had thoroughly documented the
sad plight of the Indians and so helped to create a climate in
which an avowed advocate of Indian rights, John Collier,
could be appointed Commissioner of Indian Affairs to institute
an "Indian New Deal" in the spirit of the Roosevelt Administration.

The first two of the following articles outline the detailed
plan by which Collier hoped to relieve the strain imposed on
native Americans by the Allotment Act of 1887. With the
overt goal of making Indians into small farmers, that act had
facilitated the passage of millions of acres of land out of Indian
hands and into those of whites. With the loss of their lands, Indians had fallen into a state of rural poverty and depression.

Like the goal of many other reformers, Collier's was assimilation of Indians into the "mainstream" of American life. Yet
unlike his predecessors, he sought the assent and active cooperation of the Indian peoples, and he intended that they should
be allowed to continue their traditional ways and so to proceed
peaceably and slowly toward such assimilation. Collier was as

knowledgeable about Indian affairs as any white of his period; yet it is significant that he never drew the conclusion that, since Indians were citizens (by congressional act of 1924), they already were entitled to all the rights of other American citizens, including the right to maintain as many or as much of their traditions as they saw fit. Given that citizenship rights were legally theirs, the Indians did not require new programs granting these same rights again; instead, what they required was assistance in compelling the acknowledgment of their rights from the institutions that were denying them.

Nonetheless, the Indian New Deal was to be of considerable benefit to Indian peoples, since it made a frontal attack on many of the most vexatious problems. Land allotment was stopped. Indian tribes were encouraged to organize themselves as governments that would receive formal recognition from the federal government. In all, a sizable number of Indian groups did elect to come under the provisions of the Indian Reorganization Act, although acceptance was by no means universal, because some tribes were deeply suspicious of any alteration of the status quo. Collier had not expected anything like unanimous endorsement of the Indian New Deal and in one article asserts that it would be better to have "rebellion than dry rot among the Indian groups." An editorial from *The New York Times* (December 24, 1939) expresses the sentiments of many who saw the Indians as making a comeback. The Indian population was increasing; self-help programs like the one among the Navajo were becoming successful; and the alienation of Indian lands had been stopped.

But the very success of the Indian New Deal served to reveal the interests and attitudes that had led to Indian suppression and impoverishment. As early as 1937, Burton K. Wheeler, senator from Montana, and one of the original sponsors of the Indian Reorganization Act, had become its opponent and was demanding its repeal. Some of his criticisms, and those of his allies in this struggle (for example, the American Indian Federation), will be dealt with in Part IV, "Termination," but we may note here that the ideological phrasing was that the IRA was encouraging communism and had created an authoritarian system where Indians "were herded like cattle." Wheeler proclaimed his desire for the native Americans to be encouraged to melt into the general white population and his dissatisfaction with a program that instead encouraged Indian exclusiveness and condoned communal living. Intriguingly, a similar condemnation of the IRA came from a suitably conservative Indian association, the American Indian Federation (otherwise distinguished by its ties to pro-Nazi and anti-Semitic groups, including the German-American Bund).

Trying to read behind the rhetoric, we may guess that the impact of the IRA had been deeper and greater than anticipated. Initially legislators had simply wanted to relieve Indian poverty and bring monies to their depression-ridden communities. But the IRA was doing more: it was denying to local whites the opportunities to use or gain control over Indian resources, and it was giving to Indian communities more political clout. Local white groups were becoming upset by this shift in power. Also, Indians being themselves diverse and having varied, even opposed, interests, some were bound to dislike the Indian New Deal.

The onslaught against the Indian New Deal did not come to complete fruition until after the Second World War. Meanwhile, as the United States became involved in military preparations, federal funds were diverted both from the social welfare programs of the New Deal itself as well as from the Indian New Deal. Indians themselves became involved in the war effort as soldiers and laborers. While the Great Depression had helped to shelter Indian communities, and the New Deal had helped them to reorganize themselves, the war penetrated them deeply as it did rural America generally. Neither Indian communities nor white were ever to be the same.

We should note the assumptions and fallacies inherent in the New Deal for native Americans. First, it was assumed that Indians would assimilate, even if at their own speed. Instead, what was to happen was that Indians would change, but would nonetheless retain a strong political and social sense of Indian identity. Second, there was the familiar assumption that Indians were essentially alike. Collier's personal experiences had been in the Southwest with the tightly organized Pueblo peoples for whom he had great admiration. His background did not prepare him to cope with diversity of Indian interests and preferences, some of which were individualistic or Anglo oriented. Third, the New Dealers assumed that Indians, if given the opportunity, would organize themselves into unified tribal governments that would operate by majority rule as effective forces for tribal self-help. But most North American Indian peoples had little familiarity with the Anglo system of majority rule; instead, they operated on a different organizational logic.

In the materials from the Modoc War, we noted that Captain Jack had not the political or military authority that whites accord to a chieftain. His role was more that of a spiritual leader or exemplar than of a chief executive who could enforce his wishes with the police power of a state. Indian groups operated on the basis of consensus and without coercion. When people were troubled, they met and discussed until they agreed on what should be done; if they could not reach unanimity, they continued their discussion, as no action could be undertaken. The legislative procedures familiar to whites and crystallized as "Roberts Rules of Order" permit a majority of an assembly to mobilize its strength and commit the group to action even in the face of minority dissent. Were that process to have been undertaken among a traditional Indian group (such as the Modoc of the previous chapter) the opposition would simply have withdrawn. Traditional Indians did not vote "Nay" and then accede to the will of the majority, but rather they refused to participate and their cooperation could not be enforced.

The IRA brought formal constitutions, Roberts Rules of Order, and formal judicial processes to Indian tribes; it also brought the notion of coercive government equipped with police powers. By instituting these political systems among Indian peoples, the IRA did facilitate tribal dealings with federal and state governments, but these systems impressed most Indians as being immoral, unreasonable, and dictatorial. Over the centuries and only too often have there been formulated schemes of hope and seeming merit for the improvement of Indian affairs. All have failed because they assumed that the organizational logic of Indian peoples was the same as that of the Anglos. Thus, the IRA was to create its own enemies within both the Indian and white populations.

A Lift for the Forgotten Red Man, Too. John Collier | There are in the United States today some 350,000 Indians. The majority of them live on reservations, for the most part in the Western States. They subsist chiefly by grazing and small-scale farming; a small percentage of them engage in forestry operations. On paper the Indians are estimated to possess property worth $1,500,000,000; individually they live in a state of incredible poverty, being in many tribes never far from actual starvation.

The Indians are citizens of the United States made so by a special act of Congress passed in 1924 as a gesture of gratitude for their services to the nation in the World War. Notwithstanding, Indians having the status of government wards today—that is, two-thirds of the total Indian population—cannot make contracts, cannot borrow money, cannot hire a law-

SOURCE: *New York Times Magazine*, May 6, 1934.

yer or get their own money into their hands without permission from a special government bureau, the Office of Indian Affairs.

They have no control over their tribal funds; they have no control over the white employes of the bureau who administer these funds for them. Schools have been built for them in past years, some on elaborate scale, yet so ill-advised have their educational provisions been that the illiteracy level of Indians under Federal guardianship is not less than 30 percent. The Indian death rate is just about twice that of the general white population.

It cannot be gainsaid that the Indians of our country are a most grave problem, economically and socially—and certainly from the standpoint of the national conscience, since, it is ourselves that have so reduced them from a high original level of independence and culture. Today they represent utterly helpless human material; under the present system they are at the mercy of the white man and his government.

What can the present Indian administration do about it? Without action by Congress, nothing basic. It can, however, present to Congress definite plans for reform. Briefly the problems are these: land administration, government within the tribes, education. This statement, however, does not even faintly indicate the proportions of the task.

First, the problems of land administration. The complications arising from this one phase of the Indian situation are unbelievably great. To deal with the question of Indian land administration is to deal with the economic handicap which, more than any other, has held our Indians back from progress during the years since peace with the tribes was established and which has worked toward their steady and increasing impoverishment.

Indian land administration, of course, is based on the principle of allotment. Allotment in turn is based on the idea of "whitening" the Indian. But this "whitening" has taken a wholly destructive form.

Actually, as allotment works, the process has meant giving, or allotting, to every Indian man, woman and child on a reservation a definite tract of land. This land so given out has then been held in trust for a certain period—usually twenty-five years—by the Secretary of the Interior.

It could not be sold or mortgaged during that time and it was also tax-free. At the end of the trust period, however, the guardianship of the Secretary ceased. The land became the Indian's outright, exactly as a white man's land belongs to him. And the next step was that the Indian usually lost it.

Almost invariably this happened. Either the Indian lost his tract by the well-known process of "selling for a song" to some sharp dealer or his heirs lost it after his death, because in such cases the provisions of the allotment laws have almost always made a sale mandatory.

Thus, under allotment, the Indian lands have passed at a merry rate to white men, until at the present time two-thirds of their original holdings have been lost to the tribes. Allotment was put in effect in 1887.

Added to the two reasons for land loss given above must be the government's practice of selling to the whites the so-called "surplus" lands after the allotting was completed. For the tracts parceled out to the individuals seldom consumed the entire reservation, and when the allotting was over—all Indians duly having their separate pieces—the rest was then thrown open to white homesteaders, at a fixed and extremely low price (usually $1.25 an acre), with the tribe having little or no voice in the matter, although, it should be remembered, in most cases these were lands guaranteed to the Indians forever by solemn treaties.

By these various processes the Indians have been forced to lose more than 90,000,000 acres. They own today just 47,000,000 acres, 20,000,000 of which are desert or semi-desert.

But this is not all. Added to the loss to the Indians from allotment is the loss to the government in the huge and ever-growing cost entailed in administering the allotted property. Under the allotment laws, when an Indian dies his property (if not sold) passes to his heirs, the income from it (usually rental) being divided among them. But as heirs increase the division increases, and the costs of administration mount accordingly, while the benefit of the income to the individual heirs decreases.

The proportion of Indian money thus diverted from useful channels to unproductive administrative detail is incredible. At one agency the annual appropriation is $80,000, and of this $65,000 goes to the barren administration of real estate—leaving just $15,000 for education, health, relief and all other purposes.

It may be asked what such a process of spoliation and waste has had to do with "whitening" the red man, and here one approaches the problem of government within the tribes which as it happens is closely bound up with the allotment theory. To answer this question it must be explained that the chief justification advanced for allotment by its organizers was that in destroying tribal holdings, allotment would also destroy tribal life and that by having his tribal background destroyed the Indian would become automatically white in tastes, aptitudes and attitudes.

Suffice it to note that the Indian has not become white and that the impairment of his race-old consciousness of tribal solidarity has bewildered, demoralized and discouraged him as a person, at the same time that it impoverished him. His own institutions for dealing with his local problems have been overthrown or discredited; he has been left no responsibilities as a human being, he has been autocratically ruled by a long-range authority emanating from Washington, which has controlled even the details of his personal life.

We have never given the Indian any genuine grounds for acquiring competence. We have failed to prepare him to enter into our civilization; and we have done our best to destroy his sense of belonging to his own. More, we have systematically endeavored to deprive him of any memory that he ever had a civilization or a social organization, or for that matter, even a religion. Psychologically—that is, in the cruelest sense—we have endeavored to cripple him. If he has not progressed, it is ourselves who have kept him from advancing.

The supporting evidence back of these statements is to be found in a comparison of the condition of the allotted Indians with the condition of those tribes who have escaped allotment—for since the system had been applied through Presidential discretion or by Congressional mandate, there are some tribes on which it has not as yet been inflicted. In the Southwest, for example, the Navajos and Pueblos unallotted, have largely retained their own governmental institutions and today manage much of their own property and administer their own local affairs on a tribal basis.

Excepting Indians made wealthy by oil strikes and similar accidents of chance, these tribes along with the Menominee of Wisconsin and the

Klamaths of Oregon, whose major resources are unallotted, are the most fortunate in the country. They are the most vital, the least broken and are in a general social sense, in the best condition to be found among our Indian population.

If further evidence be needed, one has only to make comparison between the tribes of the United States and those of Canada and Mexico. Both our neighbors have pursued the policy of supplying the Indian with educational opportunities and then letting him live as he chose. The result has been that the Indians of both countries have retained by choice, their tribal institutions, remolding them to meet modern conditions as they saw fit and that they have increased and prospered in reasonable proportion to their white neighbors.

The educational system extended to Indians in the United States in the past has been based on the same idea as allotment—the idea of crushing out Indian self-consciousness in the belief that white self-consciousness would somehow take its place. In the case of education, however, it was possible to apply the theory in a much more direct manner.

Briefly, the application has been as follows: to separate the child at an early age (usually 6) from the parents by sending it to a distant boarding school, where it would receive all its influence from white teachers, speak only English and associate with children gathered from many different backgrounds and localities where, in short, it would live as an uprooted thing. Usually children so transplanted visited their homes only at rare intervals, say once in three years.

There have been, too, definite efforts in some instances to implant in the children contempt for the parents' way of living, with the result that shame of race was born in them at an early age, to act as a psychological bar to normal self-expression throughout the remainder of their lives. There is certainly no extenuation for such a wrong to any individual. It can hardly be called Christian. And it should not be called American.

It may also be said of the boarding schools that they were inferior from the conventional educational standpoint. None of them was an institution of higher training; few were of high school grade. They did not fit the Indian children for life on white terms and they definitely unfitted them for life on the terms of their own people. They have been administered at a huge cost to the government, requiring at least $5,000,000 a year more than first-rate day schools would. Even numerically they have not met the needs of the Indians, as 12,000 children in recent years have had to remain without schooling, although the boarding institutions were sometimes crowded to a third beyond their capacity. In such cases, it may be added, there were resulting social and health conditions of a deplorable character.

Those are the great general problems that confront the present Indian administration. What has been done so far? A beginning only has been made.

In relation to land administration, on the bureau's initiative a temporary order was issued by the Secretary of the Interior last Summer forbidding sales of allotted lands except in emergency cases where the circumstances justified the act. Thus land loss has been halted, even though only temporarily.

In relation to government within the tribes—as opposed to long-range control from Washington—an experiment, fortuitous in nature, and almost miraculously fortunate from the point of view of the friends of the Indian, has been under way since last Summer, having as its great by-product over-whelming proof of the capacity of Indians to manage their own affairs.

This experiment has been carried out in the Indian Emergency Conservation Work program, instituted under the National Recovery Act. Under this act authorization was made for the employment of some 15,000 Indians on conservation projects on Indian lands, along lines similar to the projects carried out by the white Civilian Conservation Corps.

As soon as the authorization was made the administration laid down the requirement that all of this work—supervision as well as labor—should be done by the Indians themselves in so far as possible and that tribal councils should cooperate in recommending the projects to be carried out. The great spectacular example is the effort being carried forward on the Navajo Reservation, in cooperation with the Soil Erosion

Service of the Department of the Interior. Here thousands of Indians are employed, with Indian foremen, machinists, electricians, clerks and skilled workers of many degrees, and the outcome of the project should be the salvation of a great land rapidly becoming desert.

Similar projects, although on a smaller scale, have gone forward on most of the reservations and today more than half of the supervisory positions involved are held by Indians.

This demonstration—afforded almost by chance—has furnished dramatic proof at a crucial moment in Indian history of Indian energy, ambition and intelligence. The present administration considers that it answers the doubt as to racial capacity convincingly.

One of the acts of this administration has been to remove by order all restrictions on the right of the Indians to assemble and to observe their tribal customs and practice their chosen religions.

In relation to education, the policy of the preceding administration— that of gradually abolishing boarding schools and substituting day schools—has been carried on and accelerated. Five thousand children have already been removed from the boarding institutions, and a program of day-school building is going forward under funds obtained from the Public Works Administration.

For these day schools great hopes are held. It is desired that they become centers of Indian communal life, of Indian arts, of Indian industries and culture, ministering to the adults as well as to the young. It is also hoped that they may be taught by Indians in time. The boarding school plants, where possible, should be transformed into institutions of higher education.

What remains to be done? To insure for all time to the Indian the practice of the rights already granted him in theory—the constitutional rights of the American citizens to hold property, to engage in business and to educate himself. A bill—the Wheeler-Howard bill—designed to do this, is now before Congress.

What does it propose? First, in the matter of land, it provides that the land allotment laws be repealed, making the now temporary halting of Indian land-loss permanent. Then it undertakes to consolidate into workable units the now scattered and totally unworkable tracts which have been left to the Indians after years of selling allotments and to return to the landless Indians some portion of the area lost to them through government mismanagement.

To this end it authorizes a $2,000,000 annual appropriation, which would be used to purchase white-owned lands in Indian reservations and Indian-owned lands now in the divided "heirship" state, and also to provide land on which to colonize Indians who have lost everything and are now living in pauperism. And, to safeguard Indians against such loss in the future as they have suffered in the past, it forbids the sale of any Indian land to whites.

It would also provide for financial credit to the Indians—a privilege now almost wholly denied them—by establishing a $10,000,000 revolving fund, which would be a federal grant allocated to Indian communities to be used by them as a revolving loan fund, capitalizing the individual and group enterprises.

Then, in the matter of government within the tribes, the bill seeks to remove the Indians from the heretofore absolute control of the Indian Bureau and to bring them the privileges and responsibilities of local self-government wherever they wish to accept them. It provides that those Indians who so elect may organize communities and become chartered for any of the tasks and interests of their lives, according to their wishes and requirements. Such communities, when organized, would become instrumentalities of the federal government. It is hoped that in time they may become wholly self-governing, subject only to Congress and the Constitution, taking over gradually the functions now carried by the Indian Bureau, employing local Indian officers and giving employment to Indians in their own affairs, which are now overwhelmingly managed by white men.

The bill also creates a special Indian civil service, making it possible for qualified Indians to enter into the local Indian service, and giving the communities power of recall over local government employes. In the matter of education the bill would establish a system of loans and scholarship grants for Indians, making it possible for them to obtain the professional and technical training which their new responsibilities would require and which now they have no way of getting.

Finally, the bill sets up a special court of Indian affairs, through which constitutional rights and due process of law in matters of life and property would be insured—rights which are withheld from the Indians under the present system.

All this may sound simply reasonable, but the tragic fact is that, reasonable though it is, it is an exact reversal of historic Indian policy on every point. But who can look on the condition of the Indians today—poverty-stricken, dying at twice the white man's rate of mortality, limited in education and opportunity, hopeless, distrustful—and why not say that a reversal is indicated? Who could dare? Unless he be willing to say, "Their blood be on our heads," surely no one.

A New Pattern of Life for the Indian. Frank Ernest Hill | More than a mile above the sea level, on a plateau of the American Southwest, two hundred and fifty men are building a new capitol. It is not the capitol of a State. Its stone walls rise in shapes that are strange to most Americans; its name—Nee Alneeng—falls with a strange accent. Nee Alneeng belongs to a world far from Manhattan and Main Street. It is an Indian world, and the capitol belongs to the Navajo, now the largest of the North American tribes.

This little centre is symbolic of a new way of life among the Navajo: in fact, a new way of life for the 340,000 Indians of the United States. A year ago the Wheeler-Howard Act gave to the tribes the right to decide whether they would accept important privileges in education, self-determination and self-government. A popular vote was asked; the essential question was: "Do you want to help save yourselves?" So far 134 reservations containing 128,400 Indians have voted to come under the act, while fifty-four reservations with 83,179 Indians have excluded themselves.

Thus the Wheeler-Howard Act embodies an Indian policy far different from that pursued in the past. The Federal Government could

SOURCE: *New York Times Magazine,* July 14, 1935.

have conferred self-government upon the American Indian without asking him if he wanted it. To understand why he was asked, one must take a brief but discriminating glance at American history as it has affected the Red man.

The record may be thought of as falling into three stages. The first dates from the earliest white settlements in the Southwest and in Virginia and marks the beginning of a protracted struggle between European and Indian cultures. The struggle ended with the sporadic Western wars of the 1880's—in the inevitable defeat of the Indian. The last of the aboriginals entered United States Government reservations, and a second stage began: the government's effort to control and protect the Indian and adapt him to white American ways.

For more than fifty years this persisted. The possibility of a nomadic hunter's life for the Indian was gone; as a substitute, the government sought to educate him and make him a stock raiser or farmer. It is clear now that in many ways the system failed to protect him from cruel exploitation and yet prevented him from acting for himself. It led him to lean passively on the rather precarious bounty the government extended. Presently the Indian had suffered the loss of much of his allotted land, much of his separate culture, and had developed a deep inferiority complex with an accompanying resentment. Disease and bitter poverty menaced him. The days of his vitality seemed numbered.

The third stage may be said to have begun with a growing conviction among many thoughtful Americans that Indian life had latent strength and important cultural values and that the Indian if given the right opportunities could do what the government had failed to do: he could arrange a place for himself and his customs in this modern America. The appointment of John Collier as Commissioner of Indian Affairs in April, 1933, brought into power a leader of this trend of opinion.

Mr. Collier, slight, almost scholarly in appearance, at his desk in Washington describes what the administration is trying to do for the Indian and why he believes the new policy to be enlightened.

"In the past," he says, "the government tried to encourage economic independence and initiative by the allotment system, giving each Indian a portion of land and the right to dispose of it. As a result, of the 138,000,000 acres which Indians possessed in 1887 they have lost all but 47,000,000 acres, and the lost area includes the land that was the most valuable. Further, the government sought to give the Indian the schooling of the whites, teaching him to despise his old customs and habits as barbaric. Through this experiment the Indian lost much of his understanding of his own culture and received no usable substitute. In many areas such efforts to change the Indian have broken him economically and spiritually.

"We have proposed in opposition to such a policy to recognize and respect the Indian as he is. We think he must be so accepted before he can be assisted to become something else, if that is desirable. It is objected that we are proposing to make a 'blanket Indian' of him again. That is nonsense. But if he happens to be a blanket Indian we think he should not be ashamed of it. We believe further that while he needs protection and assistance in important ways, these aids should be extended with the idea of enabling him to help himself. We are sure that he can and will do this. But he must have the opportunity to do it in his own way. This is what we have been trying to extend to him. It is an opportunity he has not had since he entered the reservations, where he has been discouraged from thinking and acting for himself.

"It is all an educative process. Perhaps the most drastic innovation of the last two years has been our effort not only to encourage the Indians to think about their own problems but even to induce them to. Our design is to plow up the Indian soul, to make the Indian again the master of his own mind. If this fails, everything fails; if it succeeds, we believe the Indian will do the rest."

The people whom the commissioner is trying to reanimate, and to incite to this crusade for self-survival, are in one sense heterogeneous. There is no typical Indian but rather a hundred different types. These are scattered. The 220 tribes that comprise the race are to be found here and there in twenty-two States. They are of many different stocks physically, and they speak dozens of different languages.

Their cultures vary, and so does the degree to which they have adopted the white man's ways. The five civilized tribes, now in Oklahoma, were farming when De Soto discovered the Mississippi. So were the Pueblo Indians, who were also skilled weavers and master potters. On the other hand, the roving tribes of the Northwestern plains did little cultivating, and, though skillful in crafts, were esthetically far less developed. Similar differences persist today. Some Indians are competent farmers and stock raisers; others are less happy and successful in the settled life.

Some speak no English, are inexpert with tools and live in crude shelters; others have acquired modern houses and automobiles and serve as teachers, doctors, lawyers and storekeepers. Some tribes find a personal "planned economy" difficult; others, like the Hopi, are thrifty and farseeing. Unquestionably Indians generally are willing to use much of the white man's equipment and means to knowledge, but often are backward because their economic grip on life is a precarious one. Many of the tribes hold grants of land that is inferior or insufficient in extent, yet manage well with their facilities, and are deft as artisans and mechanics, sometimes eager for better tools, machinery and methods.

Underneath all their differences lie identical, unifying instincts, habits, aptitudes and spiritual feelings. Fine qualities are to be observed in almost any Indian group; artistic cleverness, tenacity, courage, dignity and a decent pride. Under the parochial control of the past, with its effort to make the Indian a white man, these qualities have shown but little. They have come out best where the Indian, as in the Southwest, has lived his own life.

In attempting to "plow up the Indian soul" and put these qualities into action, Mr. Collier has not depended on the Wheeler-Howard Act alone. This law is important; it may justly come to be regarded as an Indian Magna Carta. It repeals the Allotment Act of 1887 and so makes the further loss of Indian lands impossible. It provides for the purchase of additional badly needed land for the tribes up to a valuation of $2,000,000 a year.

It creates a revolving credit fund of $10,000,000 against which the Indians can borrow (if they accept the new law) when they have governmentally approved farm or industrial projects. This is wholly novel: the government had never previously recognized, in Mr. Collier's phrase, "the cold fact that capital in some form is needed to transform even a piece of raw land into a productive farm." There is a fund for scholarships also, and preference is given to Indians who seek positions in the Indian Service. Finally, there is the right of every tribe accepting the act by majority vote to adopt a constitution and take over most of the powers now exercised by the Federal Government.

All these privileges are important. Those providing economic and political sinews are especially significant because of the independence and self-reliance which they may develop. Yet the Indian Office regards the Wheeler-Howard Act as a step only. "It is merely a beginning," Mr. Collier points out, "in a process of liberating and rejuvenating a subjugated and exploited race living in the midst of an aggressive civilization far ahead, materially speaking, of its own. Even that beginning is oppressively difficult."

This difficulty has been recognized by the creation by the Indian Office of an organization unit of field agents and special men who will cooperate with tribal councils, business committees and special tribal commissions in framing the Constitution now permitted. The organization unit will advise the Indians, seeking to make the governments they set up both effective and legal. Definite educative work will be done to give the Indians an understanding of their new civic powers.

The possibilities in economic and political development here are dynamic. However, they follow a spirit and practice fostered since the Spring of 1933. This called for a much greater use of Indians both as officials in the Indian Service and as routine workers outside the permanent staff. The results have been notable.

In the case of the permanent staff, changes come slowly for all positions are subject to civil service rules. However, while in 1933 the Indian Office used 6,172 employees, of which 1,298 were Indians, its reduced force of 5,322 today contains 2,037 Indians. The Indians have derived other benefits by being utilized on ECW and CWA projects. Last year these workers swelled the total of government Indian employees to 19,616. This figure takes no account of the quota of 14,000 Indians in the CCC camps.

The work that Indians have done in the last two years in building roads, dams, bridges, trails and improving forest lands has been impressive. More than half the supervisory force consisted of Indians. Mr. Collier regards as important the demonstration they have given of skill, initiative and responsibility.

Beyond its successful effort to give the Indian a fair trial as a worker, the Indian Service has undertaken several specific projects of considerable importance to him. The most comprehensive of these has been going forward in the Navajo country. It touches all phases of Navajo existence: the preservation of the soil, its better use for farming and grazing, the character of the stock used, self-government, health, education, and, indirectly, art and spiritual life.

The Navajo nation, the largest of all Indian tribes, was confronted two years ago, and still is, with an economic crisis. On its great reservation in Arizona and New Mexico, with an area equal to Maryland, Massachusetts and New Hampshire combined, the tribe had developed sheep raising. In 1870 a population of 10,000 Indians was existing on its arid plateaux. From their sheep they got mutton, their chief food. From them also they took the wiry wool for the best known of native loom products—the Navajo rug. They raised a little corn. They hammered silver ornaments from Mexican silver dollars—creating the best known of all American Indian metal works. These activities sustained the tribe.

But meanwhile the Navajo increased from 10,000 to almost 50,000 and the sheep, under government encouragement, increased with the population. Carefully used, the range might have supported 1,000,000 head. But in 1933 there were 1,300,000. Furthermore, the land had long been overgrazed; experts reported its actual capacity had sunk to 550,000 head. Cropped too intensively, grass and bushes were losing their strength and were pulled up by hungry animals. Then the wind churned the uncovered soil into drifting hillocks. Rain, which falls seldom on the Navajo reservation but then usually in torrents, ran off the denuded land, carrying soil with it.

In order to live the Navajo must have his sheep. Having his sheep, he seemed doomed to economic ruin. Into this situation stepped the Indian Office. It had Emergency Conservation funds for work in the Navajo region. The office said:

"Reduce the number of your sheep. We will study how to control the destruction of the soil. We will employ your young men on government projects. We will show you how to use what water there is for irrigation. Gradually you will be able to increase your herds again. We will develop better stock for you, consuming no more but producing two-fold. In the end the land will give more than it has ever given."

In separate meetings and in their tribal councils the Navajo debated. What if the work gave out before the range was restored and the herds built back? This question is still in their minds. They have reduced their stock to 900,000 head; now they hesitate to reduce it further.

Meanwhile they have cooperated in the establishment of work projects and demonstration projects in various areas. Some are under the farm agents of the Indian Office; the greatest number are under the control of the new Soil Erosion Service. About 200 square miles of Navajo territory are now being managed as demonstration areas by this agency alone, sixty-seven of them about Mexican Springs, N.M.

In addition to the work with the land there are health and education and governmental projects in process. Schools are being built for the first time in the Navajo country. Navajo teachers will constitute the greater part of the teaching force, a new experiment. The staff of the first ten schools will consist of fifty Indians and five whites. Some instruction will be given in Navajo. The "Longhairs," the older men of the tribe, will be asked to teach the children tribal tradition, folklore and conduct of life. In health work Navajo girls are being trained as nurses to carry the fight against tuberculosis and trachoma into the remoter districts. Finally, at Nee Alneeng, twenty-five miles from Gallup, N.M., 250 Navajo workmen have been raising the walls of a new capitol which will make a centre for Navajo political life.

All activities are going forward with the agreement and participation of the Navajo, and their cooperation means a training in modern methods of work, in management, in government.

The activities of the Indian Office have nowhere been so intensive as in this many-sided development and conservation of Navajo resources. But they have been country-wide. The school program has sought everywhere to bring the Indian children into a closer relation to their homes by increasing the number of day schools and reducing the number of boarding schools. Many new schools for day use are rising—in California, in Montana, in Minnesota, in North Dakota. Economic and soil erosion work on a large scale is being pushed by the Indian Service and the Soil Erosion Service on the Rio Grande watershed, and the Indian is sharing in it.

All this is a part, with the Wheeler-Howard Act, of the new policy of setting the Indian to save himself. On the whole the response has been a revelation as to his capacity as a worker and his eagerness to lead. He has shown independence of spirit—often to the point of rebellion. The Navajo, by a narrow margin, have rejected the Wheeler-Howard Act because of unbased allegations that it would unduly curtail their herds.

But Mr. Collier, regretting such actions, prefers rebellion to dry rot. "The Indians may be confused and thrown back for a time," he says, "but it is a part of their life and education. They will win through in the end, in their own way."

If they win through it will, in the Commissioner's opinion, mean a victory for both Indian and white man. Economically independent, the

Indian will cease to be a financial burden to the nation. And spiritually and culturally he will bring something valuable too.

The new policy has already started a renaissance in Indian arts. Young Indians are painting murals on the walls of school houses and government buildings. They are studying the ancient pottery of their tribes in museums, and devising new designs and textures in their workshops. The young people are flocking to the ceremonial dances, which for a time they had avoided. This cultural revival goes hand in hand with an interest in self-government and economic independence. In Mr. Collier's opinion, it is equally valuable.

"The Indian," he says, "can use white technologies and remain an Indian. Modernity and white Americanism are not identical. If the Indian life is a good life, then we should be proud and glad to have this different and native culture going on by the side of ours. Anything less than to let Indian culture live on would be a crime against the earth itself. The destruction of a pueblo is a barbarous thing. America is coming to understand this, and to know that in helping the Indian to save himself we are helping to save something that is precious to us as well as to him."

New U.S. Attitude Stirs Indian Hopes. Frank I. Kluckhohn | Often when Americans have criticized the treatment accorded minorities in other countries, foreign critics have referred bitingly to this country's treatment of the Indian minority, but at long last those criticisms have lost much of their validity.

In great part as a result of a shift in Washington's attitude and policy toward the Indians, which started in 1924 and has received perhaps its greatest impetus during the Roosevelt Administration, the number of original Americans has increased to 351,878, as compared with 270,000 in 1900. In 1928 the Indian birth rate finally leaped ahead of the death rate, and in the last fiscal year the Indian population increased by 9,381, the birth rate exceeding that of the whites.

Behind this vital change, which offers tangible human proof that the government attitude has changed from one of suppression and elimination of the Red Man to one of aid and assistance, there is a tale of improved health conditions, with Indian babies born in hospitals instead of tepees; of better food and a cessation of wars, but most of all, probably, of a new will to live induced by the restoration of hope.

Concentrated in Five Zones

Although there are Indians in almost every State of the Union, the great concentrations are in five regions of the country. About one-third

Source: *New York Times*, December 10, 1939.

are in Oklahoma. About a quarter live in the Southwest generally, the great stronghold of full-blooded Indians. The Sioux, Blackfeet, Cheyennes, Shoshones and Arapahoes dwell in the Dakotas, Montana and Wyoming. The Chippewas are situated in the Great Lakes region of Minnesota, Wisconsin and Michigan, while, on the Pacific Coast, Indians are scattered through Oregon, Washington and California.

The form of life differs greatly as between the Indians in these far separated regions. In Oklahoma, where one-tenth of the people claim Indian blood, most of them do not live on reservations. In the Southwest generally almost all are living upon reservations, devoting themselves principally to sheep-herding. The Northwestern Indians live in a territory where white land is checkerboarded with that of the Indians and the Indian has an existence much like that of his white neighbor.

But almost everywhere, in more or less degree, the Indian has been taken advantage of. In 1887 the Indians owned 139,000,000 acres of land, much of it good. In 1933 they owned only 52,000,000 acres, much of it bad.

The Story of the Sioux

Typical in some ways is the story of the Sioux Indians on, or near, the Rosebud Reservation in South Dakota. Theirs is a grazing country and, after the buffalo were destroyed, they were without means of support. For over a decade after 1890, the government kept them on rations and did not allow them to acquire any sizable number of cattle. Eventually, when they did start cattle grazing, the World War came, white men leased their land to grow wheat, and they lived on this bounty. It soon disappeared.

These Sioux found that the leasing of two-thirds of their land to whites had broken up their communal lands, and had made it impossible for them to maintain their integrity and customs.

Under the Indian Reorganization Act of 1934, these Indians were again put in a position to handle their own affairs. Under a Federal charter, they elect representatives to a tribal council, have a constitution and are authorized as an incorporated tribe to do business with the Federal and State governments.

The government lent $50,000 to this tribe of 8,891 and the tribe, in turn, had made loans at low interest rates to cooperatives, largely engaged in cattle raising, and to individuals. Another move to make them a responsible and self-respecting community has been a Federal attempt properly to correlate their land holdings through consolidation of properties, exchanges of land with white ranchers and purchase or lease of vital areas.

Schools have been established to teach soil conservation, proper treatment of the range and livestock handling so that proper use can be made of what land these Sioux possess. With variations, because of different local conditions and tribal customs, much the same basic work has been done in other parts of the country.

Economic Difficulties

The economic problem, officials here say, is the biggest one facing the American Indian. On the Navajo reservation, for instance, the birth rate is increasing, but it has been impossible, because of the opposition of white interests, to get Congressional authorization for extending the reservation.

The government has attempted to answer this problem by teaching the Indians to make the best possible use of their land and of their resources.

Critics of the government's Indian policy make three principal charges. They hold that in plans for self-government by the Indians and in advancing credit Washington has proceeded in such a manner as to tie up the Indians in red-tape.

Another group maintains that in moving so fast to change the status of Indians, the government is stampeding and overstimulating the Red Man to a damaging extent. A third set charges that the government is spending too much money on the program.

The Indian Rides On | The fact that the American Indian is no longer vanishing was commented on in

Source: *New York Times*, December 24, 1939.

another column on this page the other day. For many years he was a victim of the white man's diseases as well as of the white man's bullets. The white man killed off his wild cattle, compelled him to change his mode of life, sold him whisky and in general treated him as though he were a cross between a criminal and a child. But the Indian continued to be fruitful, and by degrees he was allowed to share the Caucasian's sanitary and medical lore. As recently as 1928 the death rate among Indians was half again as high as that in the general registration area. Now it is close to the national average.

In part this change for the better in the red man's lot is due to a universal trend. In part it is the result of a more enlightened Indian policy, for which Indian Commissioner John Collier can take a good deal of credit. Mr. Collier strips the romance from our red brothers. They are, as he said in his 1938 report:

> *human beings like ourselves. The majority of them are very poor people, living under severely simple conditions. We know them to be possessed of all the powers, intelligence and genius within the range of human endowment. Just as we yearn to live out our own lives in our own ways, so, too, do the Indians, in their ways.*

It has long been Mr. Collier's belief that the Indian "problem" could not be, and ought not to be, solved by turning Indians into imitation white men. Some of them do succeed in adjusting wholly to the white civilization. Others find good, even in the modern world, in retaining elements of the communal and cooperative tribal life. Often this is practicable if only the tribal lands can be held intact, and Mr. Collier has done much toward that end. Since 1933 the land held in trust for the Indians by the Federal Government has increased from 49,000,000 acres to more than 51,000,000 acres. Of this total about 67 per cent is tribally owned.

The Indian of today counts many, of course, who are not full-blooded. Sometimes it is hard to determine whether a man is or is not an Indian. But, full-blooded or not, they are a good ingredient in the population. One hopes they will go on growing in numbers, salting our imported Americanism, and never quite forgetting, even under their store clothes, that they are Indians and were here first.

Indians' "New Deal" Brings on a Clash | Senator Wheeler of Montana, who was sponsor of the Indian Reorganization Act of 1934, regarded as a "new deal" for American Indians, said today he would press for repeal of the act. A bill to this effect has been introduced jointly by Mr. Wheeler and Senator Frazier of North Dakota.

Senator Wheeler's statement put him in opposition to John Collier, Commissioner of Indian Affairs, veteran critic of old-time government Indian policies and, according to some observers, the "whole future of 300,000 Indians is at stake" in the controversy.

The fundamental issue on which the commissioner and the Senator are at variance is whether Indians should be helped by the government to live in their own way on lands held in government trust, or whether they should be encouraged to enter the general white population and to live as individual family groups, in the manner of ordinary American citizens.

Mr. Collier holds that Indians should be preserved, so far as possible, in communities of their own, where they may carry on their traditional religions and racial customs and where they are "spiritually and economically" self-sufficient.

Senator Wheeler, on the other hand, says he has been informed by many Indians that they resented being "herded like cattle" on to reservations, where they are treated like "some special kind of creature."

Wheeler Cites Voting Difficulty

Explaining his attack on the bill he fostered three years ago, Senator Wheeler said he introduced it as chairman of the Indian Affairs Commit-

Source: *New York Times*, March 14, 1937.

tee without reading it thoroughly, and relying largely on the representations of its principal advocates.

"Since we passed it, we have seen that it did not do what it was intended to do," he said, "and, more than that, the Indians don't want it.

"They tell me that they want to be prepared and permitted to take their place in the world and make their way like any other American citizen.

"They want to go to the same schools and colleges, and meet life like any other American, instead of being herded off apart from every one else."

Senator Wheeler asserted that the Indian Administration discriminated against Indians who did not support the act. He said the requirement that tribes take three separate votes to adopt the provisions of the law was a complicated procedure not liked by the Indians.

The Blackfeet of Montana, although they had adopted the act, were dissatisfied with it, he went on, adding that the Flathead Indians had sent a petition bearing 500 signatures to Congress, asking to be relieved of its provisions.

Collier Cites School Figures

Mr. Collier declared that to speed migration of Indians from the older tribal communities into cosmopolitan society would mean certain disaster for at least 100,000 of them.

He stated that under the Reorganization Act about 50,000 of the 70,000 Indian school children are attending regular schools with white children, and that under the act the sum of $250,000 is made available annually to help Indians get professional training in technical schools and colleges.

"Indians detached from their native life and thrown into our modern, mechanized society, drop for the most part to the lowest social stratum, complete misfits," he declared, "while those living in their traditional tribal environment attain spiritual and cultural heights such as only tribal Indians know."

Mr. Collier said that 170 of the 230 tribes have adopted the protective provisions of the act by majority vote and are subsisting under it.

"None of them has asked that it be repealed," he asserted, "and many of the tribes which voted not to accept the act are desirous of being permitted to vote once more upon it in order to get its protectional benefits."

Two Camps Form over Indian Law | Senator Burton K. Wheeler of Montana was a sponsor of the Indian Reorganization Act of 1934. Now, asserting that he had been misled as to its real purposes, he wants the act repealed. In the current battle in Congress over the act both sides agree that the Indian should be developed as an American citizen, but the methods to achieve this end are sharply at variance.

When Senator Wheeler, who jointly with Senator Frazier has introduced the bill for repeal, submitted the original act in 1934, as then chairman of the Indian Affairs Committee, it was hailed as the "Indian New Deal."

The original act sought to stop the alienation of lands owned by the Indians and to provide for the acquisition of land for those who were landless, to stabilize tribal organizations by giving them real authority, to permit the tribes "to equip themselves with the devices of modern business organization," to establish a system of financial credit, to supply them with means for collegiate and technical training and to open the way for qualified Indians to hold positions in the Federal Indian Service.

Conflicting Opinions

Commissioner John Collier, head of the Bureau of Indian Affairs, is the principal proponent of the objectives set forth later in the Reorganization Act.

He contends that, for the most part, American Indians are not ready to be thrown into modern society without the guardianship of the govern-

SOURCE: *New York Times*, March 28, 1937.

ment, and that if the Indians are to grow to their fullest heights as individuals, and if they are to make a real contribution to our society, they must be encouraged to run their own affairs, develop their own culture and be placed on an economically self-sufficient basis.

Senator Wheeler, on the other hand, while agreeing that Indians should be developed to the best possible degree of citizenship, holds that the trend toward Indian individualism should be hastened; that they should, so far as possible, be freed from the restraints of "herded" reservation life.

Speaking of the objectives of the act in a report to the House in 1935, Commissioner Collier said in part:

"It goes back to the simple principle of treating Indians as normal human beings capable of working out a normal adjustment to, and a satisfying life within, the framework of American civilization, yet maintaining the best of their own culture and racial idiosyncrasies."

When he introduced the bill, Senator Wheeler says, he relied largely on representations of its principal sponsors.

"It has not worked out the way it was intended," he adds.

Indians' Objections

He said the Indians resented being herded together, and their representatives informed him they wanted to be free to live like any other citizens.

Commissioner Collier, on the other hand, points to the increase of Indian land holdings in seventeen States by 2,100,000 acres in three years; to Indian income from animal sales of $1,415,453 in 1938, compared with $266,698 in 1938; appropriation of $3,500,000 from a $10,000,000 revolving fund for loans to Indians, compared with average loans of $250,000 per year prior to 1938; the fact that 50,000 out of 70,000 Indian school children are now attending regular schools with whites; the availability each year under the act of $250,000 to provide higher technical education for Indians; and that despite charges of discrimination in use of funds, Indians who have not adopted provisions of the act received about $215 of government relief funds per person.

Tribes Ask Congress to Let Indians Alone | The American Indian Federation asked Congress today to let the Indians run their own affairs.

Tribal chieftains, in a sharp resolution, criticized Federal legislation designed to "help" the Indians and again attacked the administration of John Collier, Indian Commissioner.

The resolution asked Congress to stop passing laws "regulating" Indians unless specifically requested to do so by the tribesmen themselves.

Both the Wheeler-Howard Act and the Rogers Law, passed for the Oklahoma Indians, were assailed, the resolution asserting the Rogers Act "contains all the vicious communistic features of the Wheeler-Howard Act."

Delegates in a federation convention commended Senators Wheeler of Montana and Frazier of North Dakota for their work in behalf of laws sponsored by the Indians themselves.

Elderly reservation Indians, moccasin-clad and wearing feathers and blankets, nodded enthusiastically when Robert G. Bailey, Lewiston historian, praised the "Great Chief Joseph." Many of their fathers fought under the famous Joseph in the Indians' last stand against the whites in the Northwest.

Ask Indian Inquiry | Two Western Senators said today they would ask the Indian Affairs Committee on Monday to expedite an investigation of the Indian Service "with a view to taking action to remove Indian Commissioner John Collier if charges against him are substantiated."

Senator Chavez of New Mexico said:

"If evidence already brought forward is true, things are rotten in the Indian Bureau and I intend to see that Congress does something about it."

Source: *New York Times*, August 1, 1937.
Source: *New York Times*, August 8, 1937.

Mr. Chavez said a report he received today from a lawyer for a group which said it represented a majority of the Navajos in New Mexico and Arizona "compels me to bring this controversy over the Indian service to a head before the Navajos actually take to the war path."

Senator Wheeler of Montana said that he would "call the committee's attention to the mass of complaints against the Commissioner that have come from tribes in all parts of the country."

IV

TERMINATION:
Getting Out of
the "Indian Business"

During the 1950's influential groups managed to persuade significant blocs within the Congress and the general public that "Termination" was in the best interests of the Indians. What was to be terminated was the special relationship between the federal government and particular Indian tribes. That special relationship was based upon treaty provisions supplemented by congressional acts (such as the Indian Reorganization Act discussed in the previous section) as well as judicial decisions. Taking advantage of the perennial criticism of the Bureau of Indian Affairs, and appealing to American notions of individual liberty, the groups in favor of Termination argued that the federal relationship was authoritarian and an infringement of Indian rights. The best thing was for the United States to get out of the Indian business and thereby to free Indians so that they could have the same rights and privileges as other Americans.

The composition of the groups seeking Termination and the nature of their interests and philosophies have yet to be analyzed in detail. As the critics of Termination have noted, a considerable part of what was being asserted was distorted if not untrue. By the 1950's, Indians were no longer wards of the government but citizens of the United States and as free or "oppressed" as other citizens. The special relationships between Indian groups and the federal government were neither authoritarian nor based on favoritism but rather upon treaty obligations of long standing. Accordingly, they were prized by most Indians, who viewed Termination as a terrible threat, rather than a release. These being the facts, one surmises that at least some of those pushing Termination were moved not by a desire to benefit Indians but by a desire to acquire Indian resources, such as lands, timber, and minerals. Certainly one consequence of Termination was to transfer to private interests large sections of valuable lands belonging to the Menominee and the Klamath.

Whatever these special interests, the ideology that justified Termination was a combination of Anglo-conformity and assimilation. There was present among federal policy-makers a desire to cut the budget by settling finally the claims of Indians against the federal government and putting an end to the special status of Indians. Services that had been performed by the Bureau of Indian Affairs—educational, medical, welfare— were to be assumed by the states as "for any other citizens." Moreover, there have always been Americans who sincerely believed that the best thing for the Indians would be to "treat them exactly like everyone else," which would have meant ending every special governmental relationship and dispersing them throughout the general population so that they would intermarry, assimilate, and disappear. On the larger domestic scene, the activities of Senator Joseph McCarthy (Wisconsin) had made the label of "un-American" a dangerous brand that could be applied with fearful consequences to individuals or groups who differed significantly from their fellows. Surely, Indian policies had to be pure of any un-American taint.

Although Indian resources were lost in Termination, the policy-maker's philosophical or ideological goals were not realized. By the late 1960's Indian nationalists had branded Termination as a policy of great evil and were attacking white liberals for not having opposed it. The essays that follow show that this criticism was not accurate. From the very beginning there was a small handful of knowledgeable and vocal whites who analyzed the real import of Termination as a policy and opposed it before Congress and in the press. A *New York Times* editorial (April 4, 1954) is included to demonstrate that the Indians had support even from a major newspaper. The editorial writer injects an important fact by noting that the government's responsibility to the Indians has special characteristics that cannot lightly be disregarded. Many Americans are misled into believing that the Indians are receiving special treatment because of the magnanimity of the dominant society, when the historical reality is that these privileges were secured in exchange for surrender of the lands to which Indians, as the first occupants, had claim—claims that they had been prepared to defend by force, and that they yielded by treaty.

However, the editorial is best understood in chronological sequence, to which we now turn. Oliver La Farge was an individual who throughout his life was active in organizations designed to assist Indians. In "A Plea for a Square Deal for the Indians" (June 27, 1948), he reviews the situation of those peoples as it was at the close of the Second World War and thus provides a background to the controversy over Termination. Although he opposes that program, he concedes a good deal to the perspectives of Anglo-conformity and assimilation. Indians must "advance" in order to compete on equal terms in the dominant society. His basic assumption is that they will ultimately "fit in" to the larger society and thereby cease being problems. However, they should not be forced on this road but encouraged, supported, and guided by education. Thus, he differentiates himself from the advocates of Termination as much by tactics as by overall strategy and ideology.

The next two articles state briefly the position of those who wished "to free the Indians" so that they could be treated "just like everybody else." Indeed, Reva Bosone, the Congresswoman from Utah, states that Indians already *are* just like everyone else. That she was able to make a declaration which was so contrary to the facts illustrates the cultural myopia that limited the vision of Washington policy-makers during the decade.

However, it is the next four letters that are of special historical import. The former Commissioner of Indian Affairs, John Collier, a man who was knowledgeable and dedicated to Indian causes, forecasts more clearly than anyone else the disastrous consequences of Termination. Tribal resources will be lost, tribal identities will be destroyed, and instead of positive assimilation there will be poverty and personal disorganization. Drawing upon historical precedents, he shows that Indians never were benefited by policies that were supposed to "set them free."

What may also have helped to moderate the drive for Termination was the rise of modest political power and influence among Indians. Especially in the southwestern states of Arizona and New Mexico, where there were significant concentrations of Indians, and in particular in the case of the Navajo —who had the greatest numbers of any single organized tribe plus some wealth—the Indian vote and the Indian influence had come to be important. Prior to the 1950's, Indian political influence had tended to be negligible, because the population was small and scattered; and, like most impoverished peoples, Indians did not register and vote, even where they were allowed to do so. But the Navajo were led by some shrewd men, who so capitalized on their tribal political influence that Indians of other tribes spoke enviously of the BIA as having been transformed into a Bureau of Navajo Affairs.

While numerically smaller, other tribal groups also were acquiring political clout, especially when they had some wealth or resource to utilize. In a few cases, as among the Osage and the Oklahoma Cherokee, there were tribal dissatisfactions because the leadership was less "Indian" than the people, and yet had managed to gain federal recognition as the official spokesmen for the tribe. Notwithstanding, or even because of, such tribal divisions, the leadership group might be opposed to Termination because it would destroy the basis of their powers. Thus, whatever the exact mechanisms, recognized Indian tribal groups had begun to exercise political influence on the formulation of federal policies.

Following *The New York Times* editorial, to which reference has already been made, the last articles illustrate the professional base of those who were defenders of Indian rights: Dr. Sol Tax, an anthropologist, and Dr. Karl Menninger, a psychiatrist. Neither their statements nor those of La Farge and Collier stopped the federal policy, but they did help to slow its application, and they did provide ammunition and support for the National Congress of American Indians. During this decade, Indian organizations, most outstandingly the NCAI, were beginning to be recognized as the spokesmen for Indian affairs and were displacing the older, predominantly white, organizations, such as the Association on American Indian Affairs, which had been led by men such as Collier and La Farge. The Termination controversy assisted this process, for both its defenders and critics had to maintain that Indians should have authority in the making of Indian policy. By 1960, the NCAI had persuaded the incoming president, John F. Kennedy, to promise that Termination would no longer be the major policy of the federal government. And Kennedy was to appoint as his Commissioner of Indian Affairs Philleo Nash, an anthropologist and professional politician who was dedicated to the protection of Indian rights.

A Plea for a Square Deal for the Indians. Oliver La Farge | SANTA FE, N. Mex.—The latest official figures show that there are more than 420,000 Indians (including a few

SOURCE: *New York Times*, June 27, 1948.

Eskimos and Aleuts) in the United States and Alaska now under Federal supervision. The figure is surprising. In the early Nineteen Twenties when no one thought Indians important enough to be counted carefully, the official estimates ran around 250,000, and certainly for a long time we have assumed that they were rapidly dying out. Now we learn that they are not; on the contrary, full-bloods as well as mixed-bloods are increasing slightly more rapidly than our general population.

The Indians are going to be with us for quite a while, then. They are a factor in our total citizenry. Some 25,000 of them served in the armed forces in the last war—women as well as men. (A Pueblo Indian woman of my acquaintance recently accepted a Navy offer to return to the Navy as lieutenant, j.g., nurse.) Many thousands served in war industries. The Marines had a special corps of Navajos who were used to communicate by radio from ship to shore in landings—as simply by talking in their own language they used an unbreakable code. One of the men in the famous picture of raising the flag on Mount Surabachi, the one with his arm up, reaching, was a Papago, and shortly after the flag was set up, a Flathead was killed defending it. They sound like a useful and loyal people. We should be glad to have them around.

Yet in one area their situation has become so extreme as to catch public attention. Our greatest tribe, the 60,000 Navajos, is locked by illiteracy and endemic disease into a desert reservation which can hardly support half that number. Their condition has become so shocking that we now have under consideration in Congress a program which typifies what we need throughout. This program contemplates large-scale medical assistance, the building and staffing of schools for some 17,000 children now receiving no schooling, development of resources, encouragement of industries, and general economic rehabilitation which, if carried through, will change the Navajos, perhaps in a generation, from very primitive, half-starved herdsmen into a modern people, engaging in as wide a variety of gainful pursuits as the rest of us, and moving freely in the American world.

It will cost millions, perhaps 150 million before it is done—but then, the present direct relief bill for the Navajos runs to a million dollars a year, and will increase yearly unless their condition is changed.

This is an extreme example, and the remedy required is equally extreme, but in lesser degree this situation is repeated among many of the once famous Plains Indian tribes of the north, and in many other sections.

We took the whole country from the Indians, leaving them tracts of land, often the poorest there was, sometimes purely worthless, on which to try to get by. We shattered the simple and satisfactory life which they had been living, and in return we inflicted upon them a vast variety of diseases, above all tuberculosis, against which they had no immunities. Conquest, despoliation, disease and mistreatment they have repaid with loyalty and patriotism. We owe these people a debt. There is no excuse for us today to follow a course which will prolong and renew the evils of the white man's advent. The Indians deserve a square deal.

They certainly aren't getting it. The predicament of the majority of them is a combination of ignorance and poverty, with ill-health thrown in for good measure. The areas of land, whether reservations or individual holdings, which they have been able to hang on to are too small and too poor to support them as farmers and herders, even if they were taught the most modern agricultural methods. In practice, most of them follow relatively primitive methods, partly because they receive only a fraction of the agricultural extension service extended to every white man living off the land.

In all the years that they have been under our control, the majority of them has still not been brought far enough along in literacy, command of English, and understanding of our complex and often cutthroat civilization, to be able to contemplate leaving their reservations except in desperation, to sink to the lowest slum levels of white communities.

The Indian Bureau, often mistaken, often fumbling, hampered by a magnificent inheritance of red tape, is striving with entirely inadequate funds and far too few employes to bring these hundreds of thousands up across centuries of cultural evolution to a merger with ourselves. So far the result tends to be poverty and a long frustration which ends in hopelessness and the loss of the will to struggle.

One of the reasons why Indians don't get a square deal today is that the American public not only knows almost nothing about them, but is loaded with misinformation. There is the stereotype of the Indian himself, a befeathered, half-human creature of unnatural dignity with a habit of saying "ugh!"

Indians today run from very able lawyers, doctors, business men, trained nurses, to people who speak no English and still retain much of their ancient way of life, although very few now wear Indian costumes except for special occasions. They are notable for their keen sense of humor, ready laughter and fondness for singing. On the whole their greatest desire is to become completely equal to white men in general education and knowledge of the world, and to compete with them on even terms.

All sorts of wild ideas exist as to the status of an Indian and the meaning of the "reservations" on which many of the Indians live. By the exploiting of these misconceptions, millions of acres of Indian land and millions of dollars of Indian money have been stolen from them, and the drive to get the rest still goes on. It is well worth taking a little space to tell what the Indian's status really is.

The average Indian lives on a reservation. This is not a sort of large concentration camp. No one is compelled to live on a reservation. The Indians go and come as they please. A reservation is an area of tax-exempt land, owned by the tribe, or originally so owned, and held in trust for the Indians by the United States. It cannot be taxed, levied upon, or alienated. The Indians have received these tracts of land, inadequate though they are, in recognition of their inherent right as the original settlers of this country. Obviously, tax-exempt, inalienable land, even poor land, is a valuable asset.

The Indian is a ward of the United States. Originally, when we were dealing with recently conquered, resentful, warlike tribes, wardship included various restrictions upon personal freedom. Of these restrictions there remains only a law forbidding the sale of liquor to Indians, and this law works about as well as the Volstead Act did with us.

As a person, the Indian is completely free. Wardship consists in the trusteeship over the reservation, and a similar trusteeship over funds which essentially derive from the reservation or from the Indians' status as Indians—that is, such funds as royalties on oil from trust lands, or damages paid to tribes for claims against the Government. It also consists in the right of Indians to receive education, medical care and other such services from the Federal Government. Like reservations, then, wardship is not a restraint, but an asset. In fact, Indians as advanced as the late Vice President Curtis retained wardship status because of the advantages involved.

It is essential to grasp these two points, because the cry of "set the Indians free" by abolishing wardship and reservations is the standard device by which the plunderers lead well-intentioned citizens to acquiesce in new raids upon the Indian estate.

"Setting the Indians free" resulted, between 1880 and 1930, when the process was halted, in the acquisition by various devices—really legalized theft—of more than 100 million acres of Indian land. We have a bill before the Senate today, H. R. 1118, which passed the House without proper debate or hearings, to "emancipate" the Indians out of everything they have.

This bill would, in a short span of years, be booting people who speak no English, know nothing of our world, poverty-stricken primitives, out of all governmental help and protection. It would open the door to the final ruination of all the Indians' hopes. Yet the man who sponsored this bill did so in good faith—and ignorance.

Indians are citizens as well as wards. They enjoy every right of any citizen, except that in the sovereign states of Arizona and New Mexico they are denied the vote and cut off from social security by various trick legal devices. This is the action of the states, not of the Federal Government. Suits are pending in both states now to win Indians the right to vote, and the Department of the Interior has filed briefs *amicus curiae* favorable to the plaintiffs.

It would look, then, as if our Indians enjoyed special advantages. In theory they do. In certain areas, as in parts of Oklahoma, you will find Indians who by means of these aids and their own efforts have advanced themselves to complete equality with the rest of the population. In all too many parts of the United States and Alaska, however, sheer ignorance, widespread disease and wretched economic conditions hold them in a sort of slavery. That is the plight the Navajos enjoy, already described.

In Oklahoma you will find Cherokees in the cities and on good ranches, business men, politicians, professional men—and you will find several thousand Cherokees in the backwoods able to speak very little English and not long ago trying to survive on a per capita income of $34 a year.

We have had these people in our charge for anywhere from seventy-five years to a couple of centuries, and this is what we have to show for it. The usual way of dodging the blame, the shame of such a record is to talk vaguely about the wicked Indian Bureau, as though the citizens were in no way responsible for the failure of a branch of their Government. As a matter of fact, the Indian Bureau of the past twenty years has earnestly tried to help the Indians, although it has made many mistakes. It can do its work only as the people, through Congress, will enable it to do so.

There is a clear goal in our handling of our Indians. That is to give them all the education, medical care and economic assistance which will put them on their feet as healthy, well-informed, self-supporting citizens of the United States. When that is done, there will be no more need for an Indian Bureau. In fact, the Indian Bureau's own brief summary of its policy is that it is trying to work itself out of a job.

When the last Indian is ready to sink or swim in even competition with the rest of us, when we can say that our conquest of what is now the United States has brought full opportunity for a better life than the old one to all the descendants of the conquered, within the limits of their individual abilities, then we can relax. Then it will no longer be necessary to give Indians special status or special advantages.

If we destroy those advantages before the Indians are ready, we simply project them onto the relief rolls, as has been demonstrated over and over again. If we merely keep them in status quo and neglect them, we build up miserable populations who will continue indefinitely to be a drain upon the Federal purse and will increasingly become a liability instead of the very real asset which our Indians potentially are.

The greatest long-range economy we can make in connection with them is to spend enough on them now to give them the opportunity which they themselves so greatly desire. It is worth noting that each white citizen receives an average of $300 per year in services from the Federal, state and local Governments, exclusive of what is spent on the armed forces, while Indians receive an average of $166 per year from the Federal Government and nothing else. This is second-class citizenship.

We need to spend our money as an investment, planning it wisely. It surely should not be necessary to persuade Americans that every American child should go to school. We accept that. But with the Indians we need to go further, into many kinds of training toward true competence, and advice, guidance and assistance in getting themselves established economically.

Wherever the Indians have had a chance they have proved their capacity for advancement. If we will insure them all that chance, we shall get out of it in the end half a million or more (at the rate at which they are increasing now) extremely desirable fellow-citizens whose loyalty to this land goes back even farther, is even deeper, than that of any of us.

If we keep on passing by on the other side, a few of them will pull themselves up by desperate efforts. The spoilers and plunderers who never forget them for a moment will go on "emancipating" them from what few assets they have. The Indians will not solve our problem for us by dying out. They will live on, ever poorer, ever sicker, an infection in our body politic and a disgrace to our nation before the world.

Indian Commissioner Sees Tribes Treated like Other American Citizens in Future | Dr. John R. Nichols, newly appointed Commissioner of the Bureau of Indian Affairs of the Department of the Interior, told the twelfth annual meeting of the Association on American Indian Affairs, Inc., yesterday that the time would soon arrive when Indian people would be dealt with as other Americans and that all special tribal designations and treaty restrictions would be set aside.

In an informal discussion with association members at the American Museum of Natural History, he said that his few weeks in Washington after leaving his post as president of the New Mexico College of Agriculture and Mechanical Arts, had been marked by conflict with old concepts of viewing the Indians as "a race within a race, a nation within a nation." He asked for a new and more healthy point of view.

Admitting, he said, that many treaties and Federal laws were arrived at for the sole purpose of protecting the Indian people, he predicted a new era when the Indians could move within the general population "as free people," not restricted by tribal limits and Federal and state legislation.

SOURCE: *New York Times*, May 5, 1949.

House Unit Seeks Indian Point Four. Bess Furman | The twelve-member House subcommittee on Indian Affairs recently swung into a new phase of its technical assistance or Point Four approach to end wardship of the American Indian.

Representative Toby Morris, Democrat, of Oklahoma, chairman of the subcommittee said that with the passage of the revised Navajo-Hopi rehabilitation bill, he and Representative J. Hardin Peterson, Democrat, of Florida, chairman of the full Public Lands Committee, would request a conference in the near future with Senate leaders "to further Indian legislation generally."

At least twenty important Indian bills, all aimed to add to the independent status of the Indians were processed by the subcommittee and passed by the House in the first session of the current Congress, Mr. Morris said. These await Senate action.

He added that he hoped to get as many such bills through the House this session.

"Our subcommittee is agreed that wardship of the Indian should be ended," he said. "But it definitely should be a gradual process."

First Bill Was Vetoed

A section in the first Navajo-Hopi rehabilitation bill that would have put the Indians of those reservations immediately under civil laws of Arizona and New Mexico brought down a veto from President Truman.

The group urging this veto was led by John Collier, former Commissioner of Indian Affairs, long a crusader for the Indian's right to his own religion and to his own tribal customs in marriage, divorce and communal living. His group pointed to the danger of exploitation of Indian lands and property if the protection of the Federal Government should be removed.

Representative Reva Beck Bosone, Democrat, Utah, only woman

SOURCE: *New York Times*, March 5, 1950.

member of this House subcommittee, urges the right of young Indians to be Americans regardless of age groups.

"Personally, I would set twenty-five years as the maximum date for continuing wardship in any form," she said. "Meanwhile, individual Indians should be allowed to end wardship for themselves on a declaration basis."

Representative Bosone, who was a judge in her home city of Salt Lake before coming to Congress this session, traveled 1,000 miles through the Indian reservations of the Southwest last summer.

Of this trip she said:

"I came out of it with the conclusion that Indians are no different from you or me, nor do they want to be. The young GI's have come home and have told them of the world outside. They know, and they have made their parents know, that there is no chance for them unless they learn American ways.

"Indian parents no longer are refusing to send their children to American schools. They are clamoring to get them in. Personally, I'd like a limit of five years on school segregation."

Bumper Crop of Bills

There is a bumper crop of Indian legislation in the current Congress. An analysis of a few House-passed bills illustrates the trend toward an end to the phrase "a restricted Indian."

H. R. 2724, under a "decree of competency" system, would enable an Indian to manage his own affairs and property without affecting his membership on the tribal rolls.

H. R. 4025 would transfer control over Indian tribal funds to the Indian tribes. They could thus withdraw for expending funds deposited to their credit in the Treasury of the United States.

H. R. 3974 would authorize a $7,000,000 rehabilitation fund for the Standing Rock Sioux tribe of the Dakotas, described as having a strong sense of responsibility and desire to be self-supporting and a 99 per cent record on repayment of loans.

H. R. 2736 would subject Indians and Indian reservations in the

State of Wisconsin to the laws of the state by majority vote of each tribe without, however, depriving the Indians of their hunting, fishing and trapping rights or divesting the Secretary of the Interior or the tribal councils of jurisdiction over Indian tribal land.

The House committee has employed a former Western member, Preston E. Peden, of Oklahoma, to conduct a continuing study looking toward eventual removal of all restrictions on Indians and making them citizens in exactly the same sense that the rest of the people of this country are citizens.

Our   Indian   Population | *The writer of the following letter was Commissioner of Indian Affairs from 1933 to 1945.* The Bosone Indian bill (H. J. Res. 490), an Indian Bureau proposal which has passed the House and is on the Senate's calendar for immediate action, is only one component in a pattern of Indian Bureau actions.

The most recent unfolding of this pattern, a grave attack upon the corporate liberties of all Indians, also mentioned below, was characterized on Nov. 9 by the American Association on Indian Affairs as "a sweeping departure from principle and a deep incursion into paternalism. . . . A totally unwarranted interference with the enfranchisement towards which the Indian communities of this country have long and successfully worked."

In 1934 federal Indian policy was reoriented fundamentally and was incorporated in a series of Congressional acts.

Recognition of Rights
Of these statutes the basic one was the Indian Reorganization Act, which in effect was a new treaty and organic act, submitted in advance of its passage to all the Indian tribes of the country and subjected after

SOURCE: *New York Times*, December 3, 1950.

its passage to referenda of all the tribes. The core of the act was its recognition that Indians, like everyone else, needed to organize, to function as individuals through groups of their own devising, and to make their own choices as to way of life.

Also, as its core significance, the act restored the two-way, bilateral equation between the Indian tribes and other organizations, on the one side, and the Federal Government, on the other side. Supplemental enactments authorized and implemented the transfer of responsibility for Indian services to states and their local subdivisions, and in the years after 1934 this transfer, under contracts which carried grants in aid, moved ahead rapidly in Wisconsin, Minnesota, the Pacific Coast states, and school districts in many other parts of the Indian country. The tribes, as well as the Government, could embark on contractual arrangements with public and private agencies. The tribes organized themselves, within the statutory frameworks, into municipal political corporations and business corporations. Within this changed patterning of Indian affairs the long-suppressed social energies of the tribes moved into actions various, beautiful and even massive; as a single example, the Indians in their groups demonstrated that they were the best credit risks in the United States.

Attack on Achievements

It is the above-sketched changed pattern of Indian affairs, and the thousand achievements of the tribes under it, which are now under attack—they are, in fact, being silently torn to shreds through administrative actions. The silence is ended, now.

The particular action by Indian Commissioner Dillon S. Myer which was denounced by the American Association on Indian Affairs as quoted above has been an arrogation to himself of an unprecedentedly arbitrary and exhaustive control over the litigations and legal arbitrations of the tribes. Litigation and legal arbitration are essential in the defense by Indians of their property rights, business transactions and cultural rights; Commissioner Myer in effect has made these processes captive within his own office.

The most famous contest by an Indian tribe for its land and water rights, since fifteen years ago until now, has been a contest by the Pyramid Lake band of Nevada to prevent the transfer of its title to white squatters through bills promoted by Senator Pat McCarran. Never until now has the Indian Bureau yielded to this predatory drive of McCarran's.

Last month the Bureau yielded; and then President Truman moved in and canceled the surrender which Commissioner Myer had made. But the President cannot administer the Indian Bureau; and the Pyramid Lake surrender is only one item among a great many in the renewed "liquidation" and "assimilation" pattern of Indian affairs.

Provisions of Bill

Finally, a word concerning the Bureau-promoted Bosone bill must be said. This bill denies the bilateral nature of the Government-Indian relationship. It contemplates the hurried liquidation of federal responsibility to Indians, hence the destruction of that whole complex of structures built up since 1929 toward Indian self-development and dignified, high-level, true assimilation into the American stream. As introduced the bill authorizes the Interior Department to spend a quarter of a million dollars a year on personnel hired and used outside of any controls of federal fiscal and civil service law; this personnel being charged to find ways to implement the Bosone bill.

This bill was rushed to Congress within two months after Commissioner Myer and his group of new top men had taken over the Indian Bureau; was rushed out of the committees with no more than token hearings, and rushed to House enactment and onto the Senate's calendar before the tribes had a chance to even know of its existence. Will it be blocked now, in the Senate?

The predatory pressures against Indians are not sated yet, and "liquidation" and "assimilation" are stereotypes appealing to many minds. There is imminent danger. The pattern and fatality of past years is re-establishing itself very rapidly.

John Collier

Striking at Indians | *The writer of the following letter is president of the Institute of Ethnic Affairs.* The situation in American Indian affairs has entered a crisis phase. The facts should be known before, not after, the coming election. A directive from Commissioner Dillon S. Myer to all Indian Bureau officials, dated Aug. 5, occasions the crisis and also describes it.

The thirty-four-page directive of Commissioner Myer was sent to Indian Bureau personnel but not to the press, nor to the Indians or the Indian welfare groups.

In brief, the Myer directive is aimed at the destruction of federal trusteeship toward Indians, and the obliteration of that complex of achievements for and with Indians which commenced with President Hoover's Administration and became enlarged under President Roosevelt, and was continued until 1950. The document is extraordinary because it contravenes, sweepingly, statutory directions of Congress and a host of bilateral treaties, agreements, contracts and commitments which the United States and the Indians have entered into across more than one hundred years and up the years until 1950.

Directive's Purpose

The subject of Commissioner Myer's covert, if not secret, order is "Withdrawal Programming." Indian Bureau personnel are commanded to make "withdrawal," i.e., the wrecking of federal trusteeship, into the overriding objective. "We must proceed," the directive states, "even though Indian cooperation may be lacking in certain cases."

"Withdrawal" means the termination of United States educational, health and welfare services to Indians; the unilateral voiding of the Government's trusteeship toward the Indians' lands and other properties; the individualizing of much or most of the Indian corporate estate, and the casting of Indian landholdings under the local land taxes of states and counties.

The "basic methods to the development of withdrawal" already have

SOURCE: *New York Times*, October 19, 1952.

been laid down in the California Indian "withdrawal" bill which Commissioner Myer pressed for enactment in the last Congress. This California bill was the entering wedge for substantially identical bills affecting all or nearly all the Indians.

This bill empowered the Commissioner (nominally the Secretary of the Interior) to dispose, without Indian consent, of tribal lands, funds, water rights, irrigation systems and all other tribal properties; to terminate tax exemptions without application or consent of the Indians concerned; to sell or give way, in his discretion, without Indian consent, federal Indian schools, hospitals, etc., built and until now maintained for the benefit of Indians; and to prescribe, virtually without limit, rules and regulations governing Indian property and local organizations; and these rules and regulations were made exempt from review or correction in any court of law. The bill did not become law.

Commissioner Myer's Aug. 5 directive is silent as to the position of Secretary of the Interior Oscar Chapman, and of the President. Nor has the Administration either publicly endorsed or repudiated the Myer directive.

Federal Commitments

One line in the thirty-four-page Myer document mentions "treaty rights pertinent to withdrawal." Nowhere are mentioned the Congressional agreements and executive orders which have been enacted in lieu of the unwithdrawn treaties since 1872, nor the hundreds of federal commitments in the Indian Reorganization Act of 1934 and the federal constitutions and charters bilaterally established pursuant to that act. The personnel is commanded, in effect, to proceed on the assumption that the Government's contractual obligations have been or can be, through direction or indirection, voided by Commissioner Myer. That assumption is, plainly speaking, totalitarian and unconstitutional.

The oldest and also the most living, and the most profoundly buttressed, of United States trusteeship commitments is the American Indian commitment. The "pilot projects" of Point Four, now our world-wide enterprise, were the Indian projects of the Hoover and Roosevelt

Administrations; and they were hugely successful. The concentrated unilateral assault against the trusteeship obligation, now revealed in Commissioner Myer's document, concerns every citizen, and must be disturbing to every supporter of the United Nations Charter.

John Collier

Threat to Indian Rights Seen. Bill Proposing Termination of Federal Services to Tribes Opposed | In the name of "equalizing" the American Indians the Department of the Interior is sponsoring ten bills which, in the main, empower the Secretary of the Interior, without any statutory provision for the consent of the Indians' tribal governments, to terminate federal services and protections to, and liquidate the assets of, approximately 70,000 American Indians, about one-sixth of the total American Indian population.

Affording the Indians only one opportunity to be heard, joint hearings of the Interior and Insular Affairs Committee of both houses of Congress are imminent. Although the proposed measures were submitted without approval by the President's Bureau of the Budget, there is every likelihood that they will become law unless the public and the President see through the beguiling but utterly misleading slogan and take vigorous action to oppose them.

The naked intent of the "termination" bills is to throw the burdens of federal obligations to the American Indians upon the states. Two states have already declared their opposition to the assumption of any such obligations. A number of Indian tribes have already registered their bitter opposition with the Department of the Interior.

Rights and Privileges

While most Congressmen and most (we hope, all) officials of the Interior Department know that the American Indians do enjoy the status of

SOURCE: *New York Times*, February 24, 1954.

full citizenship, including the right to vote, the same old myths are being used to mislead and gain the support of a public which has only the best of intentions toward the American Indians. Even the myth that Indians may not leave their reservations has been revived. The implication is made that American Indians do not possess at least the same rights and privileges as all other citizens by utilization of the statement that American Indians should enjoy "exactly the same rights and privileges as the rest of us."

What is actually meant is that the hard-won special rights of and services to the Indians for which many of them paid and are still paying a high price in lands, lives and economic hardships should be taken from them.

The falsity of the implication that Indians enjoy only a "second-class" citizenship is shown by a statement made by the Commissioner of Indian Affairs himself only a few days ago. In a speech delivered on Jan. 21 before the Indian Rights Association the Commissioner said: "To the best of my knowledge, there are now no laws left on the federal statute books which could be rightly regarded as measures of discrimination against the Indian people."

Another implication fostered by those promoting the ten "termination" bills is that the Indians and the United States would benefit by this program. Here are the undisputed historical facts: every time (and they have been numerous) the Federal Government has sought to demolish American Indian rights or to abandon its trusteeship obligations toward the American Indians the results have been costly.

Disruption of Indian Life

On the one hand, Indian property rights were assaulted or destroyed, Indian tribal and community life was disrupted, and the Indians were demoralized and disoriented, not "assimilated"; on the other hand, administrative absolutism over Indians was intensified and multiplied, the Indian Bureau's drafts upon the Treasury increased instead of diminishing, special interests profited by the removal of the one serious bulwark protecting the Indians' property, and in many instances the Federal

Government laid itself open to claims far exceeding the cost of meeting their obligations to the Indians.

The assault against Indian rights is here the more menacing in that it is represented by numerous bills, varying, in the main, only in detail, rather than one piece of legislation, thereby potentially splintering effective opposition.

The public can insist on a firm policy that any bills affecting the American Indians must contain a provision requiring the Indians' freely given consent as expressed through their tribal governing bodies or referenda of the tribal memberships. In so insisting we will be according the Indians their equal rights to local self-government consistent with the principle of government by the consent of the governed.

John Collier

Threat to Indians Feared | As the current session of Congress draws to a close the American Indians, our oldest, most basic national minority, are again confronted by still further assaults cloaked in the guise of "emancipation," "liberation" and "equality."

Of the numerous bills introduced, at least one of which has already been enacted into law (Menominee of Wisconsin, Public Law 399), five others have already passed the Senate. (One, H. R. 303, has passed both houses, with only a conference report remaining for House agreement and another, S. 2670, is now in conference, having passed both houses in different versions.) Many others are in imminent danger of passage in a last-minute rush during the closing days of this Congress.

The real nature of this assault against the Indians' property, their local community governments and their very existence as Indians is sharply revealed by the recent article "Program to 'Free' the Indians' Advances" (*New York Times*, July 19), which reports the myths and stereotypes cur-

Source: *New York Times*, August 1, 1954.

rently employed by Senator Arthur V. Watkins and Assistant Secretary of the Interior Orme Lewis to obtain Congressional support and public acquiescence.

Rights as Citizens

As the Indians and their friends have repeatedly stated, indeed, grown weary of repeating, Indians are citizens and are at present entitled to enjoy the rights and privileges enjoyed by all other United States citizens. Indians are not "segregated" or forced to live on reservations, but are free to choose their place of residence, on or off the reservation, and to leave or return to their reservation when they desire to do so. They may sue in state courts; make valid and binding contracts; vote in federal, state and local elections; and, like other citizens, pay most federal, state and local taxes. In the words of Commissioner of Indian Affairs Glenn L. Emmons, "To the best of my knowledge there are now no laws left on the federal statute books which could be rightly regarded as measures of racial discrimination against the Indian people."

What Indians do possess are certain rights and privileges which they have secured for themselves by contract, treaty, agreement or statute, and incidental to and apart from their rights and privileges as citizens. These rights and privileges were promised them by the United States Government in return for the cession of Indian lands.

It is these rights and privileges that Senator Watkins derides as "federal windfalls." It is these rights and privileges that Senator Watkins would force the Indians to surrender, regardless of their desires and of the solemn obligations owed by the United States to the American Indian people.

End of Federal Responsibility

The real and underlying purpose of this so-called "emancipation" legislation manifestly has nothing to do with the Indians as United States citizens, or with their rights and privileges as citizens. The real objective is to end federal responsibility to the Indians, regardless of treaties, agreements and statutes, over the opposition of the Indians.

The certain result will be to destroy Indian self-help, to confuse or drive underground the cultural life of the tribe and individuals, and to open to white seizure the Indian-owned lands, forests, minerals, water-power and other assets worth billions of dollars.

What the "emancipation" legislation is now doing to the Indians, whether through racial conceit or ignorance, rather than primarily through greed, has a larger significance. The rights of each of us in a democracy can be no stronger than the rights of our weakest minority.

John Collier

Voice of the Native: Arizona's and New Mexico's Redskins Could Swing the Election in Those Two States.

Alden Stevens | This is the first Presidential election in which the Indian vote will count—and it may mean somebody's scalp.

Of the 450,000 Indians in the United States, all but about 115,000 have had the vote for many years, but the disenfranchised ones were concentrated in the only two states where their vote might really be effective. Arizona, with a total population of 749,587, has 70,000 Indians; New Mexico has 45,000 in a total of 681,187.

The Arizona State Constitution denies the vote to "persons under guardianship," and this, until 1948, was taken to mean Indians. Then two Apache war veterans carried their plea to the State Supreme Court, which decided the phrase didn't apply to Indians. The same year in New Mexico a Pueblo ex-Marine sergeant challenged the state's voting ban on "Indians not taxed" and showed a Federal district court that Indians pay sales, income and many other taxes. They got the franchise.

It was too late that year (July 15 in Arizona and August 4 in New Mexico) to do much. This is not true today. If eight electoral votes in those two states decide an election the Indians aim to deliver them, and in any

SOURCE: *New York Times*, November 2, 1952.

case there's going to be something said about who their Governors are and who are going to Congress.

A new, mostly veteran-led, sense of political power is everywhere in the Indian country, but nowhere is it so strong as in Arizona, where all tribes have combined in a state-wide Intertribal Council. When the council's chairman, a young Papago Indian, Thomas A. Segundo, told Secretary of the Interior Oscar Chapman that Arizona Indians wanted to select their own attorneys and wanted the Government to check only professional standing and the reasonableness of their fees, Chapman rescinded a new procedure setting up many other points on which the Government might reject Indian attorney contracts. Many people testified on the same matter, but there was no doubt Segundo represented the most Indians.

Segundo shrewdly began his campaign to get out the Papago vote by talking to the women. Before long there were more squaws registered than braves, and then it was no trouble at all to get the men to swoop down on the registration booths, like Hollywood warriors attacking a wagon train. The 7,000 Papagos will definitely be heard from this year.

Arizona Indians in 1950 swung the state for Republican Governor Howard Pyle. He had promised to end discrimination against them. Presently they accused him of not delivering. When Clarence Wesley, an Apache leader, politely asked him why, he called Wesley an agitator. Wesley may be a red man, but he's no red, and he didn't like it. Barry Goldwater of Phoenix, the Republican Senatorial candidate, seems popular in the Indian councils, who have been heard to complain about incumbent Democratic Senator Ernest W. McFarland.

General Eisenhower, mindful of those electoral votes in New Mexico and Arizona, dropped in at the Gallup (New Mexico) Intertribal Indian Ceremonial, heavily attended by Indians from both states, on August 10. "My own (boyhood) heroes were * * * Red Cloud, Chief Dog, Crazy Horse and Geronimo," he said. During World War II "never did I hear a complaint about the battle conduct of the North American Indian." He closed with a plea that Indians "exercise the right of universal suffrage." It was good medicine.

In New Mexico 15,000 of the 45,000 Indians probably will vote. Democratic Senator Dennis Chavez, who has done much for the Indians, is running against former Secretary of War Patrick J. Hurley who, one Indian said, has "never done anything but kiss a few papooses, who complained that his mustache scratched."

Responsibility to the Indian | Pending before Congress at this time are ten so-called "termination" bills, which would remove all special federal protection from more than 60,000 American Indians in a dozen states (including New York) and, by giving them a theoretically "equal" status with other citizens, would throw them on the tender mercies of a civilization that every lesson of history shows has used them ill. The bills would divest the Federal Government of a responsibility that morally belongs to the Federal Government and practically can still be exercised only by the Federal Government.

In those few cases where Indian tribes want and are ready for abandonment of the special federal services and removal of federal protection Congress can afford to grant them their wish. But in the many cases where those conditions do not exist Congress cannot afford to cast them adrift. Too many Indians are now suffering from hopeless poverty, chronic ill health, abject ignorance, for Congress to be promoting the "termination" of federal responsibility against their will at the present time. Too many special interests are lying in wait to take advantage of the Indians' helplessness once federal protections are removed.

John Collier, former Indian Commissioner and now president of the Institute of Ethnic Affairs, points out that virtually none of the "termination" bills requires prior consent of the Indians. The Association of

SOURCE: *New York Times*, April 4, 1954.

American Indian Affairs, headed by Oliver La Farge, says the bills "would destroy tribal governments and nullify rights assured by treaties." Of the various tribes affected by the present bills the association names several that are opposed, pointing out that many others not immediately involved are also against the program because of what they see in store for them in the future. Congress and the Administration should take full note of the interests and desires of the people most directly concerned.

Two Ask U.S. to Save Indians' Culture. Donald Janson | Two students of the frustrations of American Indians asserted today that Government policy seemed to be aimed at dooming Indian culture.

The two were Dr. Karl A. Menninger, psychiatrist of the Menninger Foundation in Topeka, Kan., and Sol Tax, chairman of the Department of Anthropology of the University of Chicago. The Menninger Foundation is concerned with research training and treatment of mental illness.

A resolution adopted by Congress in 1953 declared that it was the policy of Congress to end the Indians' status as "wards" of the United States "as rapidly as possible." The Bureau of Indian Affairs has taken the resolution as a mandate to terminate Federal supervision of tribes where possible and to push relocation of Indians to jobs off the reservation.

The psychiatrist and social scientist agreed that it was impossible to force Indians "to become white men."

They urged that the resolution be revoked in favor of a pending Senate resolution.

Dr. Menninger and Mr. Tax accused the bureau of irresponsibility and failure to try to understand the Indian point of view. They expressed themselves in an interview and on a panel at the annual convention of the National Congress of American Indians.

SOURCE: *New York Times*, October 31, 1957.

U.S. Is Criticized on Indian Policy. Austin C. Wehrwein | Prof. Sol Tax, chairman of the University of Chicago's Anthropology Department, attacked today the Administration's policy on American Indians.

"If a sink-or-swim policy is adopted," he asserted, "the Indian will simply 'float.'"

Professor Tax began studying the Fox Indians in Iowa twenty-five years ago. He outlined his views during a panel discussion at the annual meeting of the American Anthropological Association.

After the formal session, he said the Federal Government's policy began to deteriorate late in the Truman Administration and was "going from bad to worse."

The typical white man's attitude, he told the panel, is that the Indian will either die out or become assimilated.

An Example Cited

"A current example," Professor Tax said, "is the present policy of the Federal Government in attempting to withdraw from what the Indians consider obligations long incurred."

Indians object on principle to what they consider bad faith, he said. He added:

"The Indians are frightened—even paralyzed—at the prospect of losing the few services they have, and especially the school."

Professor Tax said that neither assimilation "nor its opposite are inevitable." Indians, he argued, can maintain their identity while making changes that will make them self-sufficient.

But, he added, a necessary condition would be continuation for as long as needed of "the small amount of money provided by the Federal Government for Indian education and health."

For several years the Interior Department's Bureau of Indian Affairs has encouraged Indians to leave reservations and the policy is to turn Indian education over to the states.

The association named Professor Tax its president-elect. He will become president in 1959.

SOURCE: *New York Times,* December 29, 1957.

BUSINESS, POVERTY,
AND INDIAN
COMMUNITY ACTION

A variety of modern Indian communities are portrayed in the
following essays, written by white observers during a time interval of a decade and a half, which covers the presidential administrations of Eisenhower, Kennedy, Johnson, and Nixon.
Various as are the Indian peoples, yet the observers present a
number of common themes and make a number of similar
criticisms. In this section the portraits and criticisms are those
of whites; in the section following, an Indian, Vine Deloria,
Jr., will have his say, sometimes about the very same people
(the Oglala Sioux of Pine Ridge, South Dakota). So the reader
should be forewarned that facts about Indian communities are
capable of differing interpretations.

In the introduction to the section on Termination, we referred to the organizational logic of traditional Indian peoples
and the fact that only a few white observers have been sensitive
to it. Being unaware of this logic, most observers believe that
Indian tribal governments should be effective agencies for
community development and rehabilitation, and, by so believing, they misinterpret and condemn the orientations of the
local Indians. Most tribal governments are recent creations—
dating from the Indian New Deal—and few have achieved
deep roots among the population. In a large number of cases,
local Indians do not grant real authority to the government that

whites think is theirs, but instead grant their allegiances to the local residential community of kith and kin.

Observing rural Indians, many whites judge them by whether or to what degree they are "making progress." Such observers see Indian reservations as being composed of "progressives" (who are making progress) and conservatives (who are resisting it). This judgment comes easily to men who conceive of themselves as being better—or better off—than were their parents and forebears. Seeing so little of value in their own ancestral past, they are impatient with Indians who find meaning and value in theirs, and they cannot comprehend that in North America and elsewhere are many folk who think that the best they could or should do is to be as wise and good as were their fathers and grandfathers. For such peoples, "progress" is illusionary or superficial, or at most a matter of the convenience of an automobile as compared to the back of a horse; continuity is important and fundamental. The attitude is well expressed by the Papago in Deloria's essay ("This Country Was a Lot Better Off when the Indians Were Running It"): that elderly sage sees the Spanish as having entered into his desert homeland and then as having departed; the Mexicans as having entered and then departed; now the Anglos have entered, but some time they too will depart, while "the Papagos and the mountains will always be here."

A related bias among white observers is the reference to "federal handouts" to the Indians. In almost all cases, these payments are services or monies that are made in fulfillment of treaties negotiated between the particular tribe and the government. When the federal government wanted the Indians to yield certain lands that they were occupying and defending, it promised them that if they would restrict their lives to the locale selected, they would be compensated annually for the losses so incurred. Today as observers or reporters, we may judge that the government or the Indians got the worse end of that bargain, but to refer to payments made in fulfillment of a contract or a treaty as "handouts" is inaccurate as well as in poor taste.

Occupying lands that were lacking in moisture and difficult or unsuitable for agriculture, the Mountain Ute, the Oglala Sioux, the Navajo, have each developed their own modest styles of living. In the past, they required little in the way of residences; they occupied hogans, tepees, or primitive cabins in winter, while in summer they often slept out of doors or sheltered themselves behind brush or under "shades." Their frugality and fortitude aroused the admiration of the early explorers and mountainmen who encountered them and lived among them. Since that time, many have modified their housing, but they have kept it simple and inexpensive in a fashion that should continue to elicit our admiration. Yet, instead, reformers and the government have been urging them into more conventional or suburban style residences, even when they lack the resources to justify that adaptation. Particularly is the movement unwise where water is scarce and population densities are low. Urban housing is premised on the consumption of running water in relatively large quantities; yet the costs of purification and distribution of water in arid areas may be considerable. In their desert habitat, the simple sanitary procedures of the Utes, which the reporter Seth King characterizes as "primordial," may in fact be the most satisfactory in economic and ecologic terms.

Of course, some Indians may in fact prefer the style of housing conventional to urban and suburban areas, and they may either possess the resources to underwrite such housing or, as poor people, be eligible for federal assistance in construction. Hopefully, they will be well advised in the siting and building of their houses and in the securing of financing and federal subventions; certainly they should not be the victims of discrimination in the administering of federal law.

Adjacent to the reservation areas of the Sioux, the Ute, the Navajo, and Taos are towns and cities dominated by whites. Too often, these whites think of themselves as a superior caste with the privilege of exploiting the Indians and keeping them in a subordinate status. Indians are treated as if they had few or no civil rights. The courts and police force are utilized as a way of supporting the local government by subjecting the Indians to unwarranted fines or forcing them to perform maintenance work. Under these circumstances, arrest rates reveal more about the pattern of Indian/white relationships than they do about Indian drunkenness or irresponsibility. Indeed, the process of criminal justice is often adjusted so as to relieve the Indians of portions of whatever income they receive as annuities or per capita payments.

Perhaps the most outrageous practice occurs in relationship to the schools. The federal government allots monies to schools that enroll certain numbers and kinds of Indian children, in order that special programs and services can be given to them. In many towns, the enrollment of Indian children is encouraged so that these funds can be claimed from the government, but the monies then disappear into the general budget of the school system without a trace of a program or service for Indians. Meanwhile, the Indian children are regarded as a lower caste nuisance within the schools and so are covertly encouraged to drop out; especially when there is a confrontation between the authority of the school administrator and the pride of the youngster, the latter may feel that he has been kicked out rather than that he has chosen to drop.

Symbolic of the cultural and social hurdles faced by Indian children has been the portrait of their people as presented by the mass media. When the Indian is perennially the villain and the loser, when he is ever the obstacle to the settlement and growth of the nation, then it is difficult for Indian children to develop a positive self-image. Likewise, it is also difficult for

non-Indian children to develop a balanced and moral perspective toward American history and their relationships
with those who are descended from the natives of this country. Stanley Walker's essay highlights this bias of the media, but his is a formulation of the early 1960's. By the end of the decade, Indians themselves were challenging the media, and they were no longer as supplicative as the title "Let the Indian Be the Hero," but were instructing the media that he *was* the hero and they had better set the record straight. However, this is a matter more pertinent to the selections presented later in this volume.

Bearing in mind these considerations of exploitation, bias, and social class or caste, the reader can gain from these accounts a valuable understanding of rural Indian communities and their problems.

Lo! The Rich Indian. Seth S. King | TOWAOC, Colo.

—The new Oldsmobile hardtop, its bright red sides glittering in the sunlight, was parked next to a crude sun shelter made of four poles and some freshly cut brush. One pole of the shelter abutted a makeshift corral, where four saddle horses stirred the yellow dust as they stamped at the flies. The corral was in the frontyard of a new bungalow. In the backyard was a hogan—one of the squat mud and timber huts that for centuries have housed Indians who live in the deserts of the Southwest.

This incongruous grouping of the primitive with the modern has become a common sight here at Towaoc, the village that serves as reservation headquarters for Indians of the Mountain Ute tribe.

The Oldsmobile and the new house were here because the Mountain Utes, for the first time in their troubled history, have money. The

SOURCE: *New York Times*, December 2, 1956.

corral, the brush shelter and the hogan were here because tribal roots are still deep down in the past—and because the transition from a precarious existence as wards of the Federal Government to a self-sustaining society, patterned after the white man's, is still a slow and painful one for the Mountain Utes.

Their difficulties raise a troublesome question for the United States Bureau of Indian Affairs, which under the Eisenhower Administration is aiming for eventual "termination of special Federal trustee relationships" with all the Indian tribes hitherto under Government supervision: If 690 Indians, with more than $7,200,000 among them, cannot learn to care for themselves, what chance have those without such resources?

The road the Mountain Utes are traveling might not be so long nor so twisted if they had not had to start from so far back. For more years than they like to remember they led a dubious life on the 600,000-acre reservation, set aside for them in the sun-baked southwest corner of Colorado. During that time Towaoc consisted only of a few stucco buildings and a trading post. These buildings housed Bureau of Indian Affairs officials and the Government-operated boarding school for Indian children.

The Mountain Utes themselves lived in hogans, tents or dilapidated shacks scattered through the desert scrub. A few head of livestock were their only sources of independent income. The rest came from Federal Government "issue." With these handouts they bought barely enough food and clothing to sustain themselves. Many of the tribe had never been off the reservation. Most of them spoke no English, or had any but the most elementary education. Their water supply was meager, their sanitation facilities primordial, their disease and death rates high.

Then in 1942, Towaoc's water sources dried up completely. Thenceforth water had to be hauled in by truck. Largely because of this, the school and most of the other Government services on the reservation were discontinued. The nearest major bureau offices were now at Ignacio, seventy miles to the east across Colorado's rugged mesa lands.

In this haphazard manner the Mountain Utes lived until fortune burst among them on July 13, 1950.

That day the United States Court of Claims awarded the Confederated Bands of Ute Indians $31,700,000. This money was in payment for a series of broken promises made to Ute tribes after they had been ceded 15,000,000 acres in the wild mountains of southwestern Colorado in 1868. When gold was discovered in these mountains in the Eighteen Seventies, the Indians were forced off most of their land. In the Nineteen Thirties the Utes, through lawyers they had retained, started a court action to win payment for these holdings. After sixteen years of litigation, they finally got their victory.

The three Ute tribes, the Northern Utes at Fort Duchesne, Utah, the Southern Utes at Ignacio, and the Mountain Utes here at Towaoc, divided the grant on a population basis. The Mountain Utes' share of this was $6,250,000. By 1953, when Congress finally appropriated the funds, interest had swelled the sum to $7,200,000.

At that time, there were 660 men, women and children in the Mountain Ute tribe. (Since then it has grown by thirty more.) Such a sum divided evenly among them would have yielded about $10,900 for each member. Thus a man, his wife and three children would suddenly have had nearly $55,000. For the average, poverty-ridden Mountain Ute, such affluence might well have been overwhelming.

It was obvious, both to the Bureau of Indian Affairs and to the leaders of the tribe, that some system would have to be devised for using this treasure to the greatest advantage. The problem was happily aggravated soon afterward when oil and natural gas were found on the reservation and royalties from these leases began to swell the original funds.

After many weeks of discussion, the seven-man tribal council decided upon a two-phase program. The initial step was the granting of personal cash allotments in order to improve at once the living conditions of the individual members, to teach them how to deal with the white man and to show them how to spend their money. Then, while this was taking place a program of range improvement, municipal development and public health and education was started for the tribe as a whole.

The first individual grants were made in the fall of 1953 under the council's "family plan," which provided each man, woman and child with $3,000. It had to be spent under the direction of an administrator and a purchasing agent hired privately by the tribe, and with the guidance of the Bureau of Indian Affairs.

Under this plan, an average Mountain Ute family of five now had $15,000 with which to build a house and make it livable. It could also acquire its own flocks or herds to graze on the reservation. Then, using a part of the money from the oil and gas leases, the council started another set of individual grants. This time the only restriction was that half of each grant to a child had to be placed in a trust fund for his future use. The other allotments could be spent on clothing, automobiles, travel, whisky, entertainment, or any other lawful urge the Indians might have.

The present tribal administrator, a young man named John Kelley, is reluctant to list the total amounts of these individual grants. It is known, however, that during the last fiscal year each tribal member got $600.

While these individual allocations were being made, the tribal program was started. In the fall of 1953 the Federal Government reopened the boarding school. Its operations were expanded to include a day school, which the tribe helped finance with a $30,000 expenditure. In addition, the tribe provided tuition for its children in the higher grades, enabling them to attend public school in Cortez, twelve miles north of Towaoc.

The tribal council also started a public health program. A public health nurse was hired with Mountain Ute funds, to supervise a clinic at Towaoc and to conduct a health education course.

Last, and most important, the council made funds available to reclaim and reseed the tribe's depleted rangelands and to renew the search for water.

Under the direction of Charles Whitehorn, a veteran range resources expert, a number of intermittent streams have been dammed to catch water during the brief rainy season. And the tribal council has been quietly buying up private ranches in other parts of Colorado to provide a reserve of grass and water to which herds can be moved in extremely dry years. Even so, unless the Mountain Utes succeed in tying into one of the region's existing water systems or in finding new wells on the reservation, they will be left with a problem their money can't solve.

The new money itself offered immediate release from the decaying idleness and poverty of the reservation. It provided powerful new automobiles in which to streak to Cortez. It meant breathless new purchasing power to people who had seldom seen more than a few dollars.

But it so happened that in the fall of 1953, soon after the Mountain Utes got their money, Federal laws forbidding the sale of liquor to Indians were changed. The effect of this coincidence was happy for neither the Indians nor the residents of Cortez.

In the streets of that community of 7,000, the Mountain Utes have become a familiar sight. Dressed in their bright yellow cowboy boots and wide Western hats, the men often loll in the taverns or squat against the walls of the buildings. The Ute women, still wearing their ankle-length skirts and their beads and brightly colored blouses, straggle through the stores or squat alongside their men. Too frequently in the last two years the Indians' carousing has lasted through the night, interrupted only by an occasional brawl.

In a recent fourteen-month period, 1,600 criminal cases were handled by the Magistrate's Court in Cortez and the great majority involved Ute Indians. There were mutterings from residents of Cortez. There were protests from tribal leaders, who contended that liquor was being sold to Indians who were already drunk, and that the Utes were being deliberately pushed around by Cortez police. The trouble reached its climax last fall when Colorado's Governor Edwin C. Johnson ordered a special investigation.

Suspicion of the white man has always been firmly fixed with the Mountain Utes. In the Nineteen Forties, when they were poor, they felt the white man's government—and the white man himself—had forsaken them. After they got their money and became a ready and not too discerning market this changed. But a lot of the new attention now came from the pitchmen and drummers who descended on them in droves to tap their wealth.

The movement from a desert slum into the white man's type of house was certainly a mark of progress. But for many of the older Mountain Utes it was a painful wrench from familiar roots. Some resisted all efforts to lure them out of their hogans—until a small, one-room frame house with a chimney in the center and a tiny front porch was designed. In outline, this was similar to a hogan. On this basis the tribe's elder citizens agreed to live in them.

Today Towaoc is still a jumbled collection of dwellings perched on a broiling mesa. The past three years—and more than $7,000,000—have not turned it into a model village or converted many of its people into paragons of industry.

The visitor who drives through Towaoc today finds the village has pushed outward from its original rectangle of government buildings. There are now 109 new houses, many of them painted in gay colors, tucked in with the sagebrush along a loose gridiron of five and one-half miles of gravel roads.

This property now proudly bears such names as Oyarea Coyote, Clint Badback, John Laner and Lizzie Jacket. The houses are of a conservative and practical modern design. But their newness provides some startling contrasts. In most of the yards wooden privies are still embedded at rakish angles in the desert sands. New washing machines still sit idle in the sunshine beside many houses, waiting for water to be hauled to them.

Before the Mountain Utes received their fortune their lives had little definite direction. Some, through their handicrafts and livestock, sought to better their harsh lot. But many others were content to depend on what the Government gave them.

Today there is a much clearer purpose for some of the tribal members. The rehabilitation program has given them a new outlet for their energies. Today a visitor to the reservation can see them riding their stocky, powerful ponies through the sage, moving their cattle across the range or checking their new fences. But others can still be seen taking their ease in the shade of the trading-post porch or sitting in their yards under their brush sun shelters.

The great hopes of the Mountain Utes are tied to the children who romp in the dusty yards and roads of Towaoc, and the health and educational phases of the ten-year rehabilitation program are aimed largely at them.

Since last December each tribal family has been enrolled in a group Blue Cross and Blue Shield medical plan paid for by the tribe. A kindergarten has been opened at Towaoc to give pre-school-age children a grounding in English. The school at Towaoc now has classes for the first five grades. During the past year 123 pupils attended here; thirty-five older Mountain Ute children went into Cortez, four of them to high school. The tribe expects, eventually, to send all of its school children into Cortez to study beside the white man's children.

In recent months the problems of physical assimilation with the white man have eased. There are indications that the Mountain Utes are becoming accustomed to hearing the jingle of coins in their pockets and are learning how to spend them. While Governor Johnson's investigation was inconclusive, the mere fact that it was made helped to point up the interracial problem. Since then there has been a marked decline in animosity between the Utes and the residents of Cortez. Some of the Indians, particularly the teen-age children, are now dressing more like their white neighbors and tending more and more to blend into the modern scene.

But, on the cultural level, the arguments are still raging. One faction of the tribal council wants to press toward modernity with all possible speed; another insists on preserving the tribe's customs, primitive religion and identity.

"The tribe still has the big problem of developing a positive attitude among all its members toward these rehabilitation activities," says James F. Canan, superintendent of the Consolidated Ute Agency at Ignacio. "There must be a lot more participation in the program by all the members if it's going to succeed. They have a long, long way to go. But, then, they've come a long way already."

Let the Indian Be the Hero. Stanley Walker | The television industry, already beset by many problems, complaints and disparaging comments, recently has been handed another hair shirt. And it will continue to chafe if the industry doesn't mend its ways and do better by the American Indian. The Indians, several groups of them, have risen in polite, dignified wrath and complained to the United States Government that they are not being portrayed properly by the TV industry. They undoubtedly have a point here; many people think so; and if the time were 1860 rather than 1960, there might be some scalping.

But Indian ways have changed, though it is not evident on TV, and the war whoops are now well-worded protests to the Department of the Interior, which includes the Bureau of Indian Affairs, "for persistent erroneous portrayal of inferred incidents in Indian and frontier history."

Indian tribes of Oklahoma are the complainants. Lacking bows and arrows and tomahawks, and without blood-curdling yells, the Creeks and Cherokees, through a tribal attorney, took the modern, enlightened way of dealing with the problem by sending a telegram.

So far they have had small satisfaction in the replies from the bureau, which explains that it "does not have nor want any censorship authority over the television industry . . . we understand your concern . . . we would, if requested, cooperate with responsible leaders of the industry in preparation of factual (and historical) programs."

It is possible that the Indians of today do not have any vivid or first-hand memory of how things really were, and it is quite as possible that TV viewers would consider stories of Indian life today uninteresting and inaccurate, so thoroughly have they been inured to the more violent themes. Certainly life among the Indians now would have no place in the plethora of Western TV programs.

Recently a Texas boy, visiting in Chicago, was asked—after the usual oh-ing and ah-ing over his fairly modest Texas hat (five-gallon, not ten)—"Do you have much trouble with the Indians down there?" Along with such other queries as "Do you get mail more than once a week?" and

SOURCE: *New York Times*, April 24, 1960.

"Do you have a covered wagon at home, or a Cadillac?" Is it possible such questioners don't know that some Indians, like some Texans, have Cadillacs, and seldom wear blankets while riding in them?

These questions may reveal a subconscious yearning for the old days. What boy doesn't want to trek with Daniel Boone or Lewis and Clark, hunt buffalo, or round up cattle on the vast open range with a fast horse, not a pickup truck?

It is this yearning for the apparent excitement of the old days that the TV industry believes it is satisfying with its deluge of far-fetched stories. And the youngsters, those most avid TV watchers, have come to like and expect them. There would doubtless be as much yelling from them, were the portrayals changed, as has come from the Indians. And a lot less polite.

There are many periods and areas of contact between the white man and the Indian in the early history of America. But the television script boys don't appear to know about many of them, and their needles are stuck in the same groove, so to speak—the difficulties of the Westward migration of the white man.

When producers of television entertainment were convinced by their surveys that viewers could be lured by a species of Western and Southwestern melodrama, the plot carpenters were set to work building violent action interludes, pursuits on horseback, raids and massacres, and gun skirmishes between good guys and bad guys deployed in the forests, canyons and foothills.

In the writers' desultory plotting, the Indian is the ubiquitous bad guy, or is simply dragged in for color or atmosphere. Ping! cracks the rifle, or an arrow whizzes by the lead horse, and we're off. In a few instances, the Indian is necessary to the plot; in even fewer is he a worthy protagonist—a good guy.

Thus the Indian has become a standard plot element. He was the native inhabitant of those vast areas to which the white man was bringing the benefits of his civilization—and the Indian had little use for them. Settlements and houses, schools and churches, then roads and railroads were just so much hogwash to the red man.

Most of America's early history centers around contact—inimical or friendly—with the Indian, from the Pilgrims on down. The earliest times saw constant conflict. The Indian was in the white man's way, and opposed to him, for fairly obvious reasons. Subsequently the white man and Indian became more friendly, often mutually helpful, but with most of the advantages on the white man's side. The Indian could and did teach him much more than wood lore and corn planting, and the white man profited from his lessons, though few ever learned to creep stealthily through the woods without so much as cracking one of James Fenimore Cooper's dry twigs.

Then followed more times of conflict mostly in the westward movement which is where the television boys are stuck. The white man was in effect a raider and marauder, naturally resented by the Indians whose land he was proposing to seize, whose food he cornered and wasted. The Indian did not kill for sport or out of fear; he killed for food, clothing, shelter. Eventually he was pushed off his broad lands, restrained on reservations, made sick and feeble and often shiftless, by the white man's standards, until he became, in the white man's eye, an inferior character, of an inferior race.

He resisted naturally the appropriation of his land, his hunting grounds, his supply of food, animals, water, forage. Thus the plot builders had no alternative except to present him as an obstacle—along with floods, animal predators, robbers, highwaymen and the assorted crooks, criminals, confidence men and just plain trigger-happy killers who inhabit the "Westerns."

It is true that all these things existed, but they were not the whole story. The Indians know that, and have at long last got themselves together to protest. They have a point.

In fulfilling the fundamental requirement of an interminable series of television dramas—that it bring viewers back again and again and again, so that they can be sure of getting the pitch for the skin lotion or the yummy, crispy cracker—the plotters concentrate interest in a central intriguing character: the Lone Ranger, Major Adams of "Wagon Train" or Captain Holden of "Riverboat," good guys all; and in an earlier series, the great Cochise of "Broken Arrow," a good-guy Indian for a change.

These characters are put in varying but similar situations in the TV "Westerns"—and here we go again! The ping of the rifle, the whiz of the arrow, the mad dash of the rider up McAnnally's Gulch, the fast draw of the sheriff with the handle-bar mustache.

The viewers recognize these things, and feel at home with the scene. Even in the distinctly non-Western motion picture "Around the World in 80 Days," Indians charged the puffing train, chased our hero up McAnnally's Gulch to the divide in the trail, where, to elude the shower of arrows, he went thataway. The audience roared with comfortable familiarity.

Lo! the poor Indian! He always looks the same—long, black braided hair, a band around his forehead and a feather stuck at the back, buckskin breeches with fringe, his face sometimes painted to look fierce. If he is thus adorned, he does not have to do more than say "Ugh," let out with a shriek that sounds like "Wullah-wullah-wullah," stampede the horses and fall dead at the right moment. One wise Indian, commenting on these portrayals, remarked: "If we didn't wear those feathers, they wouldn't know we were Indians."

Seldom is the Indian's own life depicted—his tent or wigwam, his adobe cliff dwelling, his home fires, his squaw or his charming children; not even his victorious return from the hunt with food for the tribe; never a successful maneuver against the white man. Rather the scenes are more often gruesome, sometimes brutal and gory. "They like 'em that way," would seem to be the excuse for all this.

Well, so they may. But possibly "they" might like to see a clever Indian guiding a white man through a forest, protecting him from some wild animal, taking him safely over the rapids of a swift river. Or even good old Squanto showing those incompetent Pilgrim Fathers how to fertilize their corn.

A proper depiction of the battle of the Little Big Horn would serve to show up General Custer, as historians now do, as a lesser man and military strategist than Sitting Bull or Crazy Horse. This might please everybody, including the Bureau of Indian Affairs, Mr. Turner Bear of the

Oklahoma Creeks, and the Russians, who are said to dote on our Western films, but, as Bob Hope reported, "with the interesting difference that the Russians cheer for the Indians."

Perhaps only time and patience is the answer. This rehash of the same old theme—ride-ride, kill-kill—must wear thin eventually (they tell me rock'n'roll is on the skids).

Then the Indian may have his day. Some far-sighted, unhurried producer may take the trouble to go into history and dig out stories that are true, have the scripts written with a smattering of intelligence and variety, and now and then let the Indian be the hero.

The Indians Want a New Frontier. Oliver La Farge | The temper of American Indians has reached the boiling point. One symptom is the American Indian Chicago Conference this Tuesday, where Indians will expound their complaints and desires.

Who are American Indians? Why should they boil, and why should the rest of us care?

There are somewhat more than half a million people of more or less Indian descent, plus some Eskimos and Aleuts, who are recognized by the Federal Government to have the legal status of Indians. Most of them live west of the Mississippi, although they have reservations also in New York, North Carolina, Florida and Mississippi.

Even so, the differences, from Point Barrow to Florida, are very great and the status of Indians and the manner in which their affairs are administered is so complex that it is impossible to write an over-all description in a short space. As a sort of sample, I shall set up that non-existent thing, a "typical" tribe and reservation, through whose history and present status can be described the outlines of what most Indians confront.

SOURCE: *New York Times*, June 11, 1961.

The Hokan Tribe now lives on the Narrow River Reservation, in the northern prairie country east of the high plains. The reservation contains some fertile bottom lands, some higher prairie, not well suited to farming, and some hilly country. It was guaranteed to the tribe by the Treaty of 1870, to hold "as long as the grass shall grow and the rivers run."

Before the arrival of the white man, the Hokans numbered about 4,000. They built permanent villages of solid earth lodges, surrounded by palisades, outside of which were fields in which the women raised corn, beans, squash and some tobacco. The men hunted deer and antelope, and every year the tribe made a trip west, living in tepees, for a big buffalo hunt.

From early in the seventeenth century, when they first were found by French traders, until after the Civil War, contact with white men caused on the whole an enjoyable florescence of their culture. Horses, metal implements, firearms, woven goods, beads, mirrors, pigments, coffee, sugar and other goods enriched their traditional life without changing it. Alcohol—sometimes available, sometimes not—enlivened it.

On the debit side, they lost a good many people from smallpox in the Eighteen Twenties. In 1855, they made a treaty with the United States in which they ceded the easternmost portion of their land. In return, the Government promised to provide an agent, a blacksmith and a farmer, and to arrange for mission schools to teach the Hokans the arts of civilization.

The chiefs who signed the treaty were pretty drunk when they did so. The Hokans, however, accepted it with equanimity. They had plenty of land, and they could not conceive of having, or giving, title to it in our sense. Land was to be used; one agreed to let certain newcomers use a portion of it; that was all.

The agents and their staffs were political appointees, badly paid. They took the jobs, mostly, for what they could get out of them. The model farm and the blacksmith's shop were run for profit, and the officials worked closely with the traders whom they were supposed to supervise and control.

Two missions were established and opened schools. They, and some agents, irritated the Indians by opposing their religion. They also caused confusion, because each denomination insisted that its version of Christianity was the only acceptable one. Nonetheless, a few children stayed in the schools long enough to learn basic English and the three R's.

Occasionally, troops camped near the Hokan villages. From them, the Hokans contracted venereal disease.

On the whole, the Hokans looked down on white men. They preached an only God, but could not agree about Him. They preached against drunkenness and prostitution, but introduced both. They preached honesty, but the traders, many agency officials and some missionaries were dishonest.

During the Civil War, regular troops all but disappeared and no military were stationed near the Hokans. In 1864, the United States had a side war with the Cheyennes, nomad Plains Indians and old enemies of the Hokans, carried on by militia regiments. One of these, coming upon a Hokan buffalo-hunting camp, attacked it on the general principle that any Indian found outside a reservation was hostile. The militia killed about 200 Indians, mostly women and children, and burned the tepees.

Minor frictions—quarrels, skirmishes and occasional killings—had occurred between Indians and whites for more than a century, but the chiefs had insisted on a policy of peace toward those peculiar people who were the source of valuable goods. Now the young men erupted. They attacked and burned a number of settlements on the land they had ceded, and cleared their territory of whites. In the process, they committed some first-rate atrocities.

As soon as the United States could spare an adequate force, it marched against the Hokans. Driven from their villages, they suffered greatly. There were only about 2,500 Indians left in the tribe that signed a new treaty in 1866, surrendering more land and earnestly promising thereafter to be good. It was not necessary to waste liquor on the chiefs this time; they had begun to have an idea of the power of the white men.

The great postwar westward migration created a strong demand for more of the Hokans' good land. In 1870, the definitive treaty was made. By then, the tribe had ceded about a million acres; it was allowed to retain half a million. At that, the Hokans were luckier than most tribes in being allowed to remain on a portion of their homeland.

The Indians' situation became steadily more and more complicated. The reservation was held in trust for them by the United States; it was tax-exempt and theoretically inalienable. As trustee, the Government had authority over the uses to which the property was put. Indians were also considered wards of the Government, and this concept led to arbitrary exercises of authority over their private lives.

Yet, within the boundaries of their reservation, they retained many elements of sovereignty, had a theoretical right of self-government, and were immune from the laws and police power of the territory—later the state—in which they resided. They were not citizens.

The buffalo disappeared; so did most of the other game. The Sioux and Cheyennes, in a last moment of glory, wiped out the notorious Colonel Custer, then were broken. The land all around the Narrow River Reservation was settled by whites who, like all good frontiersmen, hated Indians with a great and deadly hatred. Roving Hokans were sometimes shot for sport. The same man who shot a Hokan woman one day might bootleg liquor to her grieving husband the next.

In the Eighteen Nineties, Washington ordered that the Allotment Act of 1887—parceling out the tribal lands among individuals—be put into effect on the Narrow River Reservation. The ideas behind the Allotment Act were two. First, that communal ownership of land was savage, while individual ownership would create pride, self-interest and healthy selfishness, leading to Christianity, civilization and other desiderata. This motivated one group of the act's proponents. The second idea, which strongly motivated another group, was that it would be easier to pry land from individual Indians than from a tribe.

The Hokans did not favor allotment, but they were now partially dependent upon Government rations and easily subject to coercion. There were 2,000 of them. They received altogether 240,000 acres in individual allotments—held "in trust" by the Government. Their remaining 260,000 acres were declared surplus and offered for sale at 5 cents an acre, payable to the tribe.

At the same time, the Hokans were beginning to split into factions. One, sensing the source of power, formed around the agency. Others formed around the missions. Mixed-bloods were increasing—some of them children of actual marriages—and they tended to form another faction. Yet another consisted of conservatives, mostly full-bloods, who wanted to hold on to ancient ways.

A majority of the tribe became Christians of one denomination or another, but the old beliefs remained strong and were passed on to their children. There were no longer any true chiefs. The old ones were dead, and the agency fostered as replacements individuals whom it could control. Factionalism, cynicism, apathy and wry humor characterized the Hokans as they entered the twentieth century.

The peyote cult reached Narrow River. With a ritual centering upon the sacramental consumption of peyote, a plant which induces visions but is not habit-forming, the cult is a variable blend of Indian and Christian elements which has since been incorporated as the Native American Church.

It is a religion which appeals strongly to those for whom life has lost its savor. It gained many converts among the Hokans, some of whom could not, and still cannot, see why they cannot follow this ritual and that of one of the missions as well, and, perhaps, practice elements of their ancient religion to boot. The spread of peyote worship created yet greater dissension in the tribe.

Federal schools were opened on the reservation. Also, promising children were taken by force and sent to schools a thousand miles or more away, so as to break their contact with their tribe and parents. Life in the schools was characterized by drudgery, physical labor, harsh treatment, prison discipline and insufficient food. They were hotbeds of tuberculosis.

Between 1910 and 1920, Washington persuaded a number of Hokans to sell their land allotments. The official reason was that the Indians would benefit by having industrious white ranchers and farmers as their neighbors. In practice, the white men bought only the choice cuts.

Where, for instance, the allotment sold contained the only spring of water for some distance, the surrounding allotments became unusable and their owners had little choice but to lease them cheaply to the white intruder. Listlessly, the Hokans went in for leasing in a big way, living in deep poverty on the income.

In World War I, a score or more of young Hokans volunteered, as did Indians from many tribes. The principal result of military service by Indians was the enactment by Congress in 1924 of a law making all Indians citizens of the United States.

Citizens, wards, beneficiaries of a trust, with Federal responsibility for their health and education, despised by their white neighbors, possessed of partial sovereignty within the boundaries of their reservation—their real status was confusing to them and to all who dealt with them. In recent years, a series of court decisions has conclusively shown that the United States has no right of guardianship over the person of an Indian, but old habits in the Indian Service of interfering in Indian personal affairs—and, among Indians, of submitting to paternalism—die hard.

In the Nineteen Twenties, the Hokan population, which had dropped to 1,500, began to increase. The same thing occurred among tribes in all parts of the country. Just why is not clear, but today Indians are increasing at a higher rate than any other ethnic group.

Beginning in 1929, the educational system was drastically reformed. Normal contacts between children and parents were encouraged; shipping children to remote schools was stopped; educational content was increased.

This change was followed by a continuing process of placing Hokan children in local public schools. The results were mixed. In one school, teachers encouraged extreme discrimination against the young Indians; in another, the youngsters found tolerable acceptance.

After 1933, reforms in Indian affairs moved rapidly. The sale of land was stopped and the tribe was enabled to buy back a number of tracts that had been lost, thus partially undoing the damage caused by "checkerboarding" the reservation with white-owned land. Under the Indian Reorganization Act of 1934, the tribe established a government with powers specified by law, took over control of police on the reservation and set up a working tribal court.

The new Federal policy was to build advancement on Indian community strength and tribal pride. A cooperative cattle enterprise was set up, the Indians buying cattle on Government credit, and an arts-and-crafts enterprise established.

Until the Thirties, Hokans had been employed by the Indian Service only as laborers. Now they were helped to qualify for white-collar, Civil Service positions. The Indians' right to religious freedom was explicitly stated by regulation; the result was to take pressure off the peyote worshipers and bring about some revival of old, tribal rituals.

Being citizens, Hokans were subject to the draft in World War II, but many young men did not wait for it. For a time, other Hokans could find ready employment off the reservation, whereas, ordinarily, the only steady work open to them in the near-by towns had been for young women as prostitutes.

The war ended. Outside employment died away. The returned veteran, when he visited one of the near-by towns, was again just another dirty Indian. The "Indians Not Allowed" signs still showed in restaurants.

Federal policy changed again. Suddenly, the Indian cattlemen were called on to pay at 1950 prices for the cattle that had been issued to them in the Thirties. At the same time, the Government stopped making loans from the Indian revolving loan fund. The arts-and-crafts enterprise was found to be "Government in business" and was closed down.

The cure for the Indian problem, Washington had decided, was to break up the tribes and scatter their members. Seven tribes were actually "terminated"—that is, legislation was enacted ending their members' special status as Indians, including their rights to tax exemption, self-government and Federal aid—before Congress changed its mind and repudiated the policy. For several years more, however, the Indian Bureau kept pushing for termination. As a result, the Hokans, like most other tribes, became badly frightened.

The general feeling among Indians was that what was happening was what was always bound to happen. The white man would never stick with a pro-Indian policy or uphold Indian interests against those of his own race. Still, briefly, in the Thirties, Indians had experienced the heady feeling of having a voice in their own fate. They might fall back into cynicism and apathy, but underneath was anger and a harsh knowledge that, with just a little help and understanding, they could remake themselves once more into a self-reliant, self-supporting, competent people.

Today, there are 2,000 members of the Hokan tribe, of whom about half are full-blood, the others ranging from almost pure Indian to almost pure white. The last have tended to move off the reservation, even as far as Detroit. They think and live like white men, and have no interest in the future of the tribe. The desire of the overwhelming majority, however, even the mixed-bloods, is to continue to be Hokans.

Two Hokans have graduated from college and three more are attending, but most young people still drop out of high school because they find themselves unwelcome and ill at ease, lack proper clothing, need to make a little money and feel no great incentive.

The agency staff consists of a score of people, of whom three are members of the tribe. These belong to the "agency faction," and will go along with whatever the superintendent wants. He is afraid of Washington and dares do nothing bold, but he wants to help the Hokans advance themselves. His dependence on the "agency faction" and the members of one Protestant church, however, has cost him the trust of the majority. His program for the tribe did not come from the people and has aroused no real interest.

A few Hokans still control sufficient areas of land to do pretty well as cattle men and farmers. They live in shabby but decent frame houses, usually badly in need of paint. The others live mostly in one-room shacks, into which, when the wind blows hard in winter, the dry snow sifts. Dirt floors are the rule. A minority have privies; wells are shallow and unsanitary.

In front of one shack is the Sacred Buffalo Bundle, around which the aboriginal religion centers. Virtually all Hokans still look on the Bundle with awe. Many, secretly or openly, pray to it.

Every summer, the tribe puts on a bona-fide version of the Sun Dance, in which most participate with enthusiasm, regarding it as an important assertion of their identity, a restatement of their proud past. The affairs are attended by many local whites. Hokans are also hired to dance at rodeos and other functions. But they are still despised, abused by the local police off the reservation, and segregated. Apathy and frequent drunkenness are characteristic of many, especially the young men.

Last year's Presidential campaign, in the course of which Mr. Kennedy made the most detailed, thoughtful and, from the Indian point of view, acceptable statements on Indian affairs that any candidate has made in recent times, electrified the Hokans. Now, they feel, the time has come for a truly "New Frontier" for Indians, a time to make their problems and their desires known to all America, no matter how explosively.

Clearly, the betrayals of recent years are not going to be repeated: the Secretary of the Interior has appointed a special committee to recommend a new Indian policy. But that is not enough; Hokan leaders have a burning desire for a positive program, designed by them, accepted by their people, insured—they know now how—against future bureaucratic sabotage. So they are on the boil, and when they meet with other Indians in Chicago, the steam will blow.

When the following article originally appeared in the Sunday Times, it provoked a rejoinder from Amos Bad Heart Bull, then an official of the Oglala Sioux Tribal Government. He pointed out that what had occurred at Wounded Knee in 1890 was neither "a stand" nor "a battle" but a massacre by federal troops of a band of Sioux men, women, and children, who had only a few pitiful weapons. He might further have remarked that it is an insult to a brave people to characterize their slaughterers as "victorious troops," even though such verbiage was employed by a War Department eager to protect itself from censure.

In his discussions of contemporary life, Calvin Kentfield conveys useful and accurate information, except that at one point—like most observers of Pine Ridge—he loses his sense of comparison and his sense of humor. From time to time the tribal government has had its share of corrupt and incompe-

tent officers and councilmen. In this respect, it is no different
from other governments in the United States, be they municipal, county, state, or federal. If a reporter walks about Pine
Ridge town, he will have no trouble encountering articulate
critics of the tribal government; but with the same ease he
could elicit similar criticisms there or elsewhere in the United
States of the office of the presidency. The existence of such
critics and the forcefulness of their comments is testimony to a
vital democracy, so that the content of their remarks should
not be taken as descriptive of a government in the final throes
of disintegration. Moreover, the reporter should be alert to the
fact that the reservation—like any democratic community—is
divided into factions and parties, and the "outs" delight in ma-
ligning the "ins." In this case, as Bad Heart Bull comments,
the canard concerns the compensation of tribal officials: they
receive $1,800 annually rather than the $7,500 mentioned in
the essay. Whatever the sum, it is more than adequately justified by the difficulties of travel on a reservation of such great
size. Councilmen must journey regularly to the tribal offices
in the agency town of Pine Ridge, and for some of them the
trip may be well over a hundred miles, including long
stretches of poor roads. If a man has no car in working order,
the "taxi fare" charged by a neighbor may approach Manhat-
tan rates, and when one considers the grit, the gumbo mud,
and the climate, together with the difficulties that an impoverished folk have in maintaining automobiles, that fare may not
be unreasonable.

Since the tribal government was initiated in the early years
of the Roosevelt-Ickes-Collier Administration in Indian affairs,
it is a relatively new form of organization for the Sioux. Previously, their association was with their bands of kith and kin
(known as *tiyospaye*) of which there were over a dozen situated
on the Pine Ridge Reservation. Outside observers and federal
bureaucrats assume that the Oglala should have a natural and

intense attachment to the tribal government. But, since that government is a novel and alien institution, the Sioux regard it with disenchantment. They utilize its mechanisms and they participate in its forms, but they speak of it with critical detachment, and they give their allegiances to their local communities.

Dispatch from Wounded Knee.

Calvin Kentfield | WOUNDED KNEE, S. Dak.—From time to time over the years, since long before the frigid Plains winter of 1890 when United States forces armed with Hotchkiss machine guns mowed down men, women, children and some of their own soldiers in the final slaughter at Wounded Knee, the Congress of the United States has become guiltily concerned about the condition and fate of the native American Indian. The most recent manifestation of that concern is the House of Representatives Bill 10560, also known as the Indian Resources Development Act of 1967, sponsored by Representative James Haley, a Florida Democrat, and a fellow Democrat, Representative Wayne N. Aspinall of Colorado, chairman of the Committee on Interior and Insular Affairs with which the bill now resides.

If enacted, the bill would allow the Indians greater freedom in selling, mortgaging, and developing what lands they still possess, encourage them through Government loans to bring industry to the reservations, and enable them with the approval of the Interior Department's Bureau of Indian Affairs to obtain loans from private sources. Indians in general, after years of bitter experience with Congressional maneuvers and of watching the depletion of their lands despite Federal largesse, are wary of the bill's benevolence, but most of their tribal councils have chosen to go along with it, chiefly because they hope that this time around the eco-

SOURCE: *New York Times*, October 15, 1967.

nomic provisions will really work and because they figure that this is as good a bill as they can get at this time.

Out where the battle of Wounded Knee took place, however, the tribal elders are decidedly unenthusiastic about the bill and its Government backers. "We know they mean well," says Johnson Holy Rock, the chairman of the Tribal Council of the Oglala Sioux at Pine Ridge Reservation in South Dakota. "Their intentions in putting forth this bill are undoubtedly of the best, but they don't understand the Indian mind, and we here at Pine Ridge have simply said we won't accept it, we want to be left out, we're not ready for it, we know we'd lose more than we'd gain and we've lost too much already."

And Brice Lay, the chief of the Pine Ridge Agency of the Bureau of Indian Affairs to which an Indian must apply in order to sell or lease his land, says, "We here at the bureau know, and the council knows, that if a piece of land comes up for bids, a non-Indian's going to get it." He pointed to a chart of the reservation that showed 42 per cent of the land already in white hands. "The Indians have first choice," he went on, "but very few of them can afford it, not even the council acting for the tribe as a whole. It's simply going to go out of Indian hands, and there's nothing on earth we can do about it."

The ever-diminishing land is almost the sole source of subsistence for the inhabitants of the Pine Ridge Reservation—or, more colorfully, the Land of Red Cloud—which is the seventh largest of the 300-odd reservations in the United States. It stretches for 90 miles east from the Black Hills and about 50 miles from the northern Badlands south to the Nebraska line.

In the eastern part some of the land is fertile enough to bear wheat, oats, safflower and the like, but 99 per cent of this farm land is now and forever in the hands of the white man. The rest of the reservation consists of rolling short-grass prairie land, an enormous landscape divided into four parts: endless green grass, tall blue sky, low ridges of ponderosa pine, and a constant rustling, sighing wind. Through these great plains wander cottonwood-shaded creeks such as Bear in the Lodge, Potato, Wounded Knee, and the twisted White and Cheyenne Rivers. In the summer, thunderclouds build up towers on the far horizons and the sun may produce temperatures of 120 degrees; in the winter, the creeks become ice and blizzard winds such as those that froze the bodies at the massacre of Wounded Knee into such baroque and unusual shapes can bring the thermometer down to 40 below.

U. S. Highway 18 passes east-west through the southern edge of the reservation. There are miles and miles of good black-top roads kept in repair by Indians working for the Interior Department road service; and there are miles and miles of roads that are no good at all. There are modern boarding schools exclusively for Indian children as well as local public schools and a Catholic mission school, outlying clinics and a good free hospital with doctors, surgeons, dentists and a psychiatrist. There are churches of all kinds (40 per cent of the Indians profess to be Catholics and more to be Protestants, but the old beliefs still lie heavily in their souls). There is an American Legion Post, a Lions Club, a Ladies' Aid, a P.T.A. and a Boy Scout troop. Nearly all of the Sioux (or Dakotas, their own pre-reservation name for themselves) speak English as well as their native Lakota dialect, and there are still a few medicine men around, like old Frank Fools Crow who usually presides over the annual Sun Dance. The center of nearly everything—government, society, law and order, education—is Pine Ridge, a town of 1,256 people close enough to the state line to have a "suburb" in Nebraska, Whiteclay, center of shopping (three supermarkets) and entertainment (bars and dance halls).

On this reservation live, in one fashion or another, nearly 10,000 Teton Sioux of the Oglala tribe. They are not the poorest nor the richest of the country's Indians. The Hopis and some of the Apaches of the Southwest are poorer, and the inhabitants of the Aguacaliente Reservation in Southern California, who more or less own Palm Springs, are richer, to say nothing of those few tribes that have oil wells. But the Oglalas range from a state of imminent starvation to fair affluence.

On the reservation itself, unemployment is 43 per cent, so some of the younger people go elsewhere for summer work. There is a new factory at Pine Ridge that employs about a hundred people to make "handmade" moccasins. A fishhook factory near Wounded Knee employs nearly 200 more, and a few more work for the Bureau of Indian Affairs. Most of the businesses—filling stations, grocery stores—are owned by whites, and the rest of the Indians work for white ranchers or live off the land which they work themselves or lease to white ranchers. The land, though it belongs to the Indians, is held in trust by the Department of the Interior, which takes care of all the leasing arrangements and issues checks to the owners each month from a computer in Aberdeen.

Aside from Interior Department employes and a few Indian ranchers, the average annual income per family is less than $900. The 34 members of the Tribal Council, however, have voted themselves a yearly salary of $7,500, paid out of proceeds from tribal lands under grazing leases. "Those earnings are supposed to be divided up amongst us all," one man told me, "but we ain't none of us seen a penny of it for years." Most of the money, of course, goes into the operation of the tribal government, which has charge of all municipal services—police, fire and courts—as well as the maintenance of lawyers in Rapid City and Washington to represent the tribe in all higher dealings with the Government, such as House Bill 10560. Though technically wards of the Federal Government under the guiding thumb of the Bureau of Indian Affairs, the Indians, since 1924, have enjoyed the rights and privileges of full American citizenship, including the right to fight in Vietnam and the privilege of paying income taxes. They enjoy some extra privileges as well, such as untaxed land.

"We try to help them," said Brice Lay in his office in the new air-conditioned bureau headquarters in Pine Ridge, "to make the best possible use of the land they have, but it's very hard." Like most of the non-Indian (the bureau does not use the term "white man") employes of the bureau, he is intensely sincere in his desire to help the Indian become a white man. "Here in Pine Ridge most of the people live fairly well, but you go out on the reservation—the way some of those people live!" He made a gesture of despair. "No one should have to live that way."

And, indeed, out on the windy treeless tracts of the reservation, at the end of two dirt ruts across the prairie, will be a one-room shack, possibly a log cabin, possibly a frame house walled in tarpaper, for a family of six, eight, ten people and surrounded by a circle of old car bodies that, like the bodies of U. S. soldiers killed in a battle of olden times, have been stripped and mutilated and left to rot where they lay. An outhouse nearby. No electricity, no running water. A monthly ration of rice, flour, powdered milk, peanut butter, margarine, lard, raisins, oatmeal, corn-meal, potted meat, dried beans, dried peas, bulgar and rolled wheat, plus $50 in cash from Welfare. This kind of poverty engenders horror, pity and disgust in the Anglo-Saxon breast, but all the Oglalas are not that badly off, and many of them simply don't want some of the amenities that the Great White Father insists they must have, if possible, for their own good.

"We had one old woman out on the reservation," Brice Lay said, "that was all by herself and living in a tent, so we found a house for her, but she wouldn't move in. She said she'd die if she lived in a house, that the air in a house was bad air. Oh, she was stubborn. But finally," he concluded with a tone of great satisfaction, "we got her in there."

Out at Wounded Knee about two miles from the general store and post office lives a man in his late fifties, his wife, two married sons, six grand-children, three dogs, two cats, some hens and a rooster. He is a full-blood, very dark, though his wife is not. He owns a section of land (640 acres) through which runs Wounded Knee Creek and on which graze about 200 head of cattle and 60 or 70 horses. He has a field of alfalfa which, this year, because of the late rains, is exceptionally rich and high and, when I visited him, was ready for cutting. There are tall shade trees along the creek, plenty of water, and a small field of sweet corn nearby.

He and his wife and one orphaned grandchild live in a very old, one-room cabin with a shade, or "squaw cooler" (though "squaw" is an insult-ing word these days), a kind of summer house made of poles and pine boughs that keep off the sun but let the breeze come through, making it a comfortable outdoor kitchen and sleeping place during the hot months. His sons and their families live in small asphalt-shingled houses on either side of the parental house. One son is a cowboy and works the section, the other works at the fishhook factory over the hill. Standing to one side at the edge of the alfalfa is a two-hole outhouse.

They carry their water from the creek, build their fire with wood and light their lamps with kerosene. They walk to the store and back, as they have no car. They are well and presumably happy. They are members of the Native American Church who use peyote, the hallucinatory cactus, in their services, during which, under the spell of the drug, they chant and sing and pray to God that the day will come when all men will be at peace and all men will be brothers. Not half a mile from this man's house reside the bones in a mass hilltop grave of the victims of the massacre of Wounded Knee.

Though a Peace Sacrifice was the climax of this year's Sun Dance— "Richard 'Buddy' Red Bow," the posters read, "17 years old, member of the Oglala Sioux tribe, will pray for worldwide peace by performing the traditional Sun Dance worship. Red Bow will pierce his flesh and offer his blood, praying for the safety of American Servicemen and a peaceful speedy end to war in Vietnam"—the Sioux were not always a peaceable people.

"Sioux" is short for "Nadowes-sioux," which is French for "Nadowessi," which is Chippewa meaning "little snakes" or, in other words, treacherous enemies. The Sioux fought everybody—the Chippewa, the Crow, the Cheyenne, the Kiowa and the white man after he came pushing onto the plains, stealing, pushing, lying, slaughtering the buffalo, always pushing. In 1866, Red Cloud, "the first and only Indian leader in the West to win a war with the United States," said to a Colonel Carrington, come to open a road to the Montana goldfields, "You are the White Eagle who has come to steal the road! The Great Father sends us presents and wants us to sell him the road, but the White Chief comes with soldiers to steal it before the Indian says yes or no! I will talk with you no more. As long as I live I will fight you for the last hunting grounds of my people."

Red Cloud and Crazy Horse, Custer's Last Stand, Sitting Bull and Big Foot, and the final slaughter at Wounded Knee! After all that misery, bravery, and bloodshed, the Sioux, romanticized by the white man, became the Ideal Indian, the Mounted Warrior in War Bonnet, the End of the Trail, the Indian at the Medicine Show, the All-American Buffalo-Nickel Indian.

The last treaty the Sioux made with the United States Government (1868–69) set aside nearly half of South Dakota, including the sacred Black Hills, and part of North Dakota as the "Great Sioux Reserve." But white men discovered gold in the Black Hills (as Johnson Holy Rock said to me, "The Indians still don't understand gold, it's a white man's concept and the white man just can't understand that"), so an Act of Congress in 1877 removed the Black Hills from the Indians' reserve. Later, another act divided what was left of the "Great Sioux Reserve" into five reservations with still more loss of land, settling the Oglalas at Pine Ridge. It is no wonder, indeed, that the Indian leaders look twice and twice again at Acts of Congress.

The Indian Bureau demands at least one-quarter Indian blood as a prerequisite for donating its paternalistic blessings—but the Pine Ridge Tribal Council has never been able to decide upon who is and who is not an Indian.

"The Tribal Council is ridiculous," said a man I shall call Edgar Running Bear because he has asked me not to use his real name. "Two of them are stupid women who have not even had a sixth-grade education, one of them is a hopeless alcoholic, and they're all prejudiced."

We were sitting in Edgar Running Bear's house in one of the several new Pine Ridge subdivisions financed by the Public Housing Authority and built by Indian labor against the fierce objections of half-a-dozen union leaders. It is a two-bedroom house, pink and white, with a carport and a front lawn like millions of others all over America. In the living room were two modernistic armchairs, a huge radio-phonograph-television combination set in the corner. On top of the TV stood a vase of plastic flowers and on the wall opposite the picture window hung a small imitation tapestry of a roaring tiger printed in lurid colors on black velvet.

It was a hot day and through the open windows we could hear the drumming and amplified chanting of one of the bands, the Oglala Juniors or the Sioux Travelers, who had gathered at the nearby campground for the four-day Sun Dance celebration, a kind of county fair, carnival and tribal get-together combined with ancient ritual which was just then beginning. The celebration is an annual rite that Edgar, at one point in our conversation, referred to scornfully as a reversion to primitivism, though he later took his children over to the campground to ride the Space-Mobile.

"Why do you say they're prejudiced?" I asked. "Against whom?"

"Against the mixed bloods."

Both Edgar and his wife, and indeed most of the population of the reservation, are mixed bloods. The classic face of Red Cloud is seldom seen. Johnson Holy Rock himself is three-quarter Oglala and one-quarter Scotch-Irish. I mentioned this fact and elicited only a shrug from Edgar.

"Do you find," I asked, "that white people on the reservation or off it show prejudice toward you because you're Indians?"

"Oh, yes," Edgar's wife said quickly. "They move onto our land, look down their noses at us, and complain about our laws and our dogs and—"

"When I go off the reservation," Edgar broke in, "I expect to abide by the ways of the people there. It doesn't bother me, if we don't get served one place, we'll go someplace else, but you could go staggering drunk down the main street of Rushville [Rushville, Nebraska, the nearest town of any size] and nobody'd look at you, but if I did—well, not me because being a policeman they know me—but if an ordinary Innun did the same thing he'd be in jail so fast . . ."

I related an incident I had witnessed in a restaurant-bar in Rushville. The television had been giving news of the aftermath of the Negro riots in Detroit and the waitress had said, "I know it's a funny attitude to take, but if one of them come in here, I just couldn't serve him. I don't know what it is, but—" Then she had given a little laugh and said, "But nobody kin accuse me of racial prejudice because I feel the same damn way about the dirty Indians."

There was a moment of silence while the drums beat at the Sun Dance grounds.

"Well," Edgar said, "that's the kind of thing you run into."

"Well, us Innuns aren't prejudiced against the niggers," Edgar's wife said. "Of course, I wouldn't want my daughter to marry one any more than I'd want her to marry a full-blood."

Edgar, slouching deeply in his armchair, gave the living room wall a kick with the side of his foot. "Look at this damn house," he said. "It's coming apart already."

"That's why we send our kids to public school instead of the B.I.A. Innun school," his wife went on, "because we don't want them to grow up with nothing but Innuns."

"To live here, to live this life we live here," Edgar said, shaking his head, "you have to be half-drunk all the time."

Until 1953, it was, as a Klamath Indian friend of mine once explained, "against the law to feed liquor to Indians." It's still against the law on Pine Ridge because the members of the tribe voted for a dry reservation, though in the "suburb" of Whiteclay there are bars and dance halls that get quite lively on a Saturday night or just after the computer has issued the Mother's Aid or Welfare check.

In those resorts, there is, as well as drunkenness, a great deal of laughter and joking and horseplay; the Oglala is a friendly and, at times, very witty creature. He loves athletic games and plays them well, and his manual deftness makes him an excellent carpenter, machinist or technician if he takes the trouble to develop his talents and possesses the courage to go into the outside world and exercise his skills. One of the commonest reasons, of course, for Indian apathy toward Government training programs is that once an Indian learns a white man's trade there is no place on the reservation where he can exercise it. He has to leave his home and relatives and work in some foreign place, and he doesn't want to. The sponsors of H. R. 10560 eagerly point out that the bill will help relieve that condition.

In one Whiteclay bar, I met a fat jolly Oglala lady who, although she has an excellent secretarial job with the bureau, also creates fine tomahawks for the ever so slightly increasing tourist trade. She has three daughters who are or are becoming registered nurses, one son who has a Ph.D. in sociology and is working with other Indians in Nebraska, and a young son who is a good-for-nothing drunk. She knows Edgar Running Bear very well.

"Pooh! You can't believe a word Ed says," she said, although she allowed that the council was, in fact, incompetent and overpaid and that Johnson Holy Rock was unfair in his recommendations for loans. In general, she felt, "the Innuns on the reservation were a passably contented lot and pretty much satisfied with the way the Bureau was handling their affairs."

"This is our place," she said. "Some of us go away, but an awful lot of us come back. See those two boys over there in the ball caps? They've been in Oakland, California, making good money, but they've come back."

I asked them why they had come back. One of them laughed and said, "Hell, I don't know. I guess to play baseball."

Johnson Holy Rock told me that he had been to Washington and explained to the Interior Department people that the chief complaints they have against the Government were that the Government treated them like digits instead of human beings, that it didn't understand the Indians' attachment to their people and their land, and that the Indians themselves didn't yet understand the white man's notion of business and money and private property. "We're not ready to be let out on our own," he had told them, "but treat us like people instead of numbers."

I remarked that all of us, not just the Indians, were victims of the official digital computer, that we were all cards full of little holes. "We've given up," I said, but this time he didn't understand, because he means to go right on trying to keep his people what they are, more so than any other Americans I know—human beings. But I'm sure that one day he, too, will give up just as Red Cloud, in spite of his vow to fight for his lands forever, gave up, finally telling his people in tones of scornful irony:

"You must begin anew and put away the wisdom of your fathers. You must lay up food and forget the hungry. When your house is built, your storeroom filled, then look around for a neighbor whom you can take advantage of and seize all he has."

That was the way, he said, to get rich like a white man.

To the Editor:

We were rather disturbed by the tenor of Calvin Kentfield's "Dispatch From Wounded Knee," October 15. The article was condescending and, we believe, demeaned a people who warrant fairer treatment.

SOURCE: *New York Times,* November 19, 1967.

The subtitle states that "Wounded Knee is where the Sioux made their last great, but unsuccessful, stand against the westward-migrating white man." Wounded Knee was not that at all. Chief Big Foot's band had earlier been disarmed by the Seventh Cavalry and was in the process of completing a peaceable trek to the Pine Ridge Reservation. Approximately 300 unarmed men, women and children were massacred by Hotchkiss machine guns as they passed through the draw at Wounded Knee.

Secondly, the article seems to suggest that each of the 34 members of the Tribal Council voted himself a yearly salary of $7,500 "paid out of the proceeds from Tribal lands under grazing leases." This is incorrect. The 34 members of the Tribal Council each receive $1,800 per year, which covers the considerable expenses involved in attending numerous tribal meetings at Pine Ridge. Some Tribal Council members must travel more than 100 miles to attend.

Finally, the image of housing at Pine Ridge was exceedingly misleading. It was suggested that subdivisions in Pine Ridge are not unlike subdivisions in other parts of America. This is public housing for low-income families and does not conjure up the idea of carports and front lawns "like millions of others all over America." The image presented in your article is one of bourgeois, middle class; but there are many Indians at Pine Ridge who opt for their proud Indian heritage rather than consider television and a can of beer as a way of life.

We hope you can set the record straight. The Oglala Sioux, after all these years, deserve at least this fair shake.

AMOS BAD HEART BULL,
Fifth Member, Oglala Sioux Tribal Council

HOWARD KAHN
Pine Ridge, S. D.

VISTAS in Navajoland. **Gertrude Samuels** | FORT DEFIANCE, Ariz.—A few sheep and dogs were nosing among the litter and sparse grass of White Mesa, a barren moun-

SOURCE: *New York Times*, August 11, 1968.

taintop on the Navajo reservation here, when Carolyn Domsic paid the Martin family a visit. Carolyn is 22, a blonde registered nurse from Cleveland, Ohio, and a VISTA volunteer. The Martins and their nine children live in a frame house and a hogan (ho-gahn), a six-sided windowless building of earth, logs and grass; they have no electricity, no running water, no sanitary facilities.

Three of the children, barefoot, ragged, ran to meet "Marble Eyes," as they call tall, blue-eyed Carolyn. She examined their tongues and ears and cleaned the sores on their feet. Mixing English and Navajo words, she soothed them as they struggled and cried. Their young mother, in red jacket and long cotton skirt, hurried up, complaining— the children had fever, she had no aspirin. Carolyn provided some.

Aspirin and cough medicine are the only medical supplies that VISTA (Volunteers in Service to America) gives Carolyn to work with. She wrote to family and friends and obtained medicated soap, neomycin and other basic supplies. Carolyn feels it would be preferable to have a doctor's supervision in her work, "but there isn't a doctor up here," she says, adding with her cool smile, "I don't think anyone's going to sue me."

Carolyn Domsic arrived on the reservation last December. She is one of 36 men and women from VISTA who are seeking to bring domestic Peace Corps benefits to the American Navajo. And though she is succeeding to a greater degree than many of her colleagues (she has, for example, been elected to the Community Action Committee of her district, a rare honor and reward for her achievements), she has known the frustrations that have plagued the three-year-old project since its inception.

In theory, the VISTA Navajo program is both practical and idealistic; in practice, it has been rather less than perfect. Progress has been held back by the basic distrust of the Indian for the white man, by the immaturity of some of the volunteers and by a multitude of bureaucratic confusions.

More than 11,000 Americans have entered VISTA since it was established by the Economic Opportunity Act of 1964. The total number

of volunteers working on projects and in training this month—5,000—
is 20 per cent greater than a year ago, when the total was 4,257. They
are serving on some 450 projects in 49 states (only Mississippi has refused volunteers) and the District of Columbia, Puerto Rico, the Virgin
Islands, Guam and American Samoa. VISTA assigns volunteers only to
communities that request them. The basic guideline of service is
philanthropy in the best sense: to help the poor help themselves. Vistas,
as the volunteers are known, go chiefly to poverty areas in city and rural
ghettos, in migrant worker camps and to Indian reservations. In New
York, they work in settlement houses, with tenant organizations, with
existing agencies on alcoholism and addiction problems. In Oregon,
they work through the Valley Migrant League with seasonal farm workers on adult education and community self-help ideas. At Queen Li-
liuokalani Children's Center in Honolulu, they tutor teen-age dropouts.

Under its legislative mandate, VISTA can theoretically take anyone
18 years of age and older, without regard to the person's skills, experience or motivation. But in fact, because of unhappy results with some
early recruits, VISTA's professional evaluators are now looking chiefly
for persons who have both an honest "commitment" and particular
skills in such areas as teaching, nursing and community organization.
This has led to a rate of acceptance of only one in every eight applicants;
it has also decreased the percentage of 18- and 19-year-old Vistas from
10 per cent to 2 per cent. As one VISTA official put it: "We're not looking for the psychological dropout from the university, or the person who
is looking to 'find himself' and sees VISTA as some sort of group ther-
apy." Neither is VISTA looking for young men whose main motivation
is to avoid the draft—though the Selective Service System has determined that the volunteers' work is in "the national interest" and draft
boards have generally granted Vistas deferments. Sixty-four per cent of
the current VISTA crop are between the ages of 20 and 24; 51 per cent
are male; 78 per cent have attended college.

Certainly, Vistas do not volunteer to get rich. They receive a basic living, travel and medical allowance and a $50-a-month stipend that is

paid at the end of a year's service, in a lump sum. Service is for a year, with an option to re-enroll. The volunteer starts his training with a week or two of courses and discussions on "The Culture of Poverty," followed by four weeks of on-the-job training in poverty areas and on Indian reservations where he lives and works at the actual poverty level. The training is calculated to test volunteers' ability to handle "cultural shock" and to think and plan creatively—and about 18 per cent of those who start don't finish. VISTA cannot afford not to be selective: it receives many more applicants and project invitations than its $30-million budget can handle.

The program on the Navajo reservation here is one of the most difficult and dramatic that VISTA has undertaken. The Navajo tribe is the nation's largest, with 115,000 members living on some 25,000 square miles of Federal land, chiefly in Arizona but overlapping into New Mexico and Utah. Together with the other "first" Americans—there are 300 Indian tribes, numbering 600,000 people—they are, tragically, the last Americans in terms of health, education and economic well-being.

The typical Navajo family still lives in the hogan; it has perhaps 50 sheep, earns less than $500 a year to pay for a limited diet of mutton stew, fried bread and coffee; there is little grazing land. In some communities the unemployment rate stands at 80 per cent. Infant mortality is high, and adult Navajos have an average life expectancy of 45 years.

An ancient Navajo prayer begins, "Now I walk with Talking God . . . /With goodness and beauty in all things around me as I go," and this is still in some ways the land of James Fenimore Cooper's "natural man" where the Indian lives at one with the wilderness. The immense russet, rock sculptures of the desert, the sacred mountains that ring sage-floored valleys, the treeless places where sheep, goats and horses scratch for food, are steeped in legend. For "The People," or Diné as they call themselves, are deeply religious, with a powerful reverence for their gods whose spirits are to be found in animals, in mountains, in all the manifestations of nature. According to their "origin myth," The People first lived far below the earth's surface until they were driven upward by a flood. When they were "discovered" by the Spanish in the

17th century (and given the name Apaches de Navajó), The People were already a great tribe.

In 1863, the tribe was nearly annihilated by Col. Kit Carson, who invaded the area to put a stop to a rash of Indian wars; the surviving Navajos were held captive at Fort Sumner, New Mexico, for more than three years. In 1868, just a century ago, the Federal Government signed a Treaty of Peace with the tribe, restored its original lands and provided a supply of sheep. Since then, the tribe has remained at peace—separate from, but far from equal to, the dominant white society.

Most of the Navajo's contacts with the white man, until fairly recently, have been through the agency created as "trustee" for all 50 million acres of Indian lands in 25 States—the Bureau of Indian Affairs (B.I.A.) in the Department of the Interior. B.I.A.'s large staff, which is responsible for the economic and social well-being of reservation Indians, has long been under fire for its paternalism which, in effect, kept the Indian dependent on handouts from the Great White Father. In spite of billions of dollars appropriated for activities, under B.I.A.'s supervision, the Indians fared so poorly that the Senate Interior Committee has described their condition as a "clear indictment of past programs and policies pursued by the Bureau."

The B.I.A. is represented here by the Navajo Agency in Window Rock. But since World War II, The People have been taking over a larger measure of self-government. A Navajo Tribal Council is mainly responsible today for a tribal code of law and for administration of tribal matters. It has representatives from the reservation's 100 political districts, known as chapters, and meets in Window Rock about four times a year in a small, handsome building which resembles a miniature U.N. General Assembly.

Under the guidance of Raymond Nakai, chairman of the council, the tribe operates on an annual budget of about $20-million. The money comes mainly from oil well royalties (about $13-million a year), from Navajo-run motels and from tribal arts-and-crafts projects. The Tribal Council uses this income to operate some social services and public works, and has invested in such projects as a sawmill and an electronic parts factory to provide jobs for the people. But the tribe has its financial problems. Says one tribal official: "If we keep operating this way on a deficit, we'll probably go broke by 1975."

With the signing of the Economic Opportunity Act in 1964, the council promptly sought help. On April 7, 1965, the council created its own Office of Navajo Economic Opportunity (O.N.E.O.), which received a Federal grant of $920,400. Another sum of $1.5-million was approved for its Neighborhood Youth Corps program.

Council Chairman Nakai had previously asked Peter MacDonald, a Navajo, to return to the tribe. MacDonald, now 39, who holds a degree in electrical engineering from the University of Oklahoma and was a project engineer on the Polaris missile for Hughes Aircraft Company in Los Angeles, returned to help evaluate and implement the tribe's programs. He became O.N.E.O.'s executive director in May, 1965, and received authority from the tribe to bring 50 Vistas to the Navajo reservation.

Today MacDonald directs 10 different anti-poverty programs for O.N.E.O., including a community alcoholism treatment program and a Headstart (child development) project. The guiding principle for all is in sharp contrast to the old B.I.A. paternalistic approach: The people down at the "hogan level" are given the responsibility for deciding what help they need most, and for initiating their own programs.

But the transition is not easy. Navajos are not accustomed to responsibilities, and their suspicions of the white man are deep and historic. The only whites The People have known are the B.I.A. agents, who had tried to wash the Indianness out of them and their children; the Public Health Service officials and the missionaries, most of whom rarely let the Indians make decisions of consequence.

Tom Atcitty, the VISTA supervisor here, is a stocky, forthright Navajo of 31, proud of his ancestry, with a bachelor's degree in social studies from Taylor University in Indiana. Much of VISTA's work, he says, has been to overcome the Indians' distrust and to make them understand the purposes of the program. When they were first told that Vistas were coming to help, some were frankly enthusiastic about getting free labor from the white man for a change and thought, "Here's a chance to get me a white slave"—someone to haul wood or carry water (which must usually be transported from the reservation's few springs). Some chapter leaders were under the impression that they were getting a custodian for the chapter house.

Most Vistas assigned to the Navajos receive, in addition to the standard six weeks of training, two to three weeks of instruction in the Navajo language, history and mores at the University of Oregon. About 80 per cent of the Navajos speak no English, and it is taught here today "as a second language."

Some of the current crop of Vistas started work last December, others are finishing a year of service. They are involved chiefly in programs encompassing education (for children and adults), health, homemaking and sanitation, they also do liaison work between the outside community and the reservation. But in some areas, much of their effort is devoted to just getting themselves accepted. The Vistas live generally in teams of two; though one member of a team may be a teacher and the other a nurse, they tend to help each other out—the need is so great, and the problems so forbidding.

The Red Mesa chapter lies in all its rocky remoteness near Four Corners (where the states of Arizona, Utah, Colorado and New Mexico meet), a spine-breaking drive of several hours north from tribal headquarters at Fort Defiance. A population of 1,000 persons lives there, mostly on tribal and state welfare.

"Ya at' eeh!" ("Hello!") was the greeting Tom Atcitty and I received from Jo-Anne Nola, a pretty, dark-haired VISTA teacher from San Jose, California. Jo-Anne, 23, arrived on the reservation in December, along with her partner, Carolyn Domsic, the nurse from Cleveland. The two girls were on their way to an adult education class in a small room of Mrs. Jessie Blackwater's house.

Mrs. Blackwater, buxom, good-natured and businesslike, is also their landlady—they pay her, at their own insistence, $20 a month rent for their hogan. And, as it turned out, she is also their "adopted mother."

Six Navajo ladies, wearing the traditional high-necked, colorful blouses, ankle-length skirts (there are no miniskirted Navajos) and head scarves, were already seated on the iron cot and straight chairs, laboriously trying to print English in their workbooks. They had walked to class from miles around to study their second language.

The two Vistas sat among the women, guiding this woman's hand—"I just want to learn how to write my name down," Mrs. Sally Lee insisted—or helping that woman to draw letters of the alphabet. The class worked in hushed absorption for about an hour. At last Mrs. Lee, her strongly seamed face beaming with satisfaction, printed, by herself, "S A L L Y L E E."

"Yes, they are good teachers," Mrs. Blackwater later said in her own rather good English, "but," she added with a twinkle, "they should learn Navajo, too."

The girls self-consciously joined in the general laughter.

We went by pickup truck over dirt roads to a slightly more advanced adult education class in another private home. Half a dozen women sat weaving rugs on large wooden looms. The rugs would be sold later through the trading posts. The women greeted the Vistas with shy smiles. Some left off weaving to sit in a semicircle before a blackboard where Jo-Anne slowly chalked in large letters: "I want to buy some . . ." (The Navajos are beginning to accept English for use when they go shopping.)

Jo-Anne went to where Mrs. Alice Nelson continued weaving while her baby on a cradleboard slept beside her on the floor. Jo-Anne watched first with immense tact. Clever fingers tugged this way and that at the fine wool strands. "That's so perfect, Mrs. Nelson," she said. "Now can you pause and join us? We're going 'shopping.' "

It brought a smile. "Yes, okay," said Mrs. Nelson. She brought her baby with her to the semicircle.

Jo-Anne enunciated loud and clear as she printed away, the women now repeating after her: "I want to buy some bread . . . milk . . . vegetables . . . fruit . . . sugar." One or two women could not pronounce the sibilants for lack of teeth.

During the days that I spent with these Vistas it became clear that the two girls had been taken to the Indians' hearts. Both are from comfortable, middle-class homes. Here, they live in a red-clay hogan, without electricity, running water or refrigeration. One day after class Jo-Anne hugged Mrs. Blackwater, teasing her: "Since the day we got here, Mother's been trying to get us married to Navajo boys!" "Maybe she can marry with a Navajo," Mrs. Blackwater retorted. "She's like a Navajo, that's why."

In fact the Vistas on the reservation do little dating. One reason is that the Indian families might get the wrong impression as to why Vistas are here—especially single young women who are not missionaries. The girls do kid each other in private. A goat or three horses is a typical Navajo dowry, and Jo-Anne will sometimes call to her partner, "Here come the three horses, Carolyn."

Why did they volunteer?

"I had wanted to get involved to try to bring about some positive change, I suppose," said Jo-Anne. She had tutored Mexican-American students back in Santa Clara, and her parents supported her in VISTA service, too—"if the people want you there." Carolyn added: "All my life my parents have given me a lot, and I just want to share what I know."

Jo-Anne had had "absolutely no training materials" to start her teaching project; she had finally begged a few adult education books from the county welfare office and had bought some colored paper, workbooks and pencils with her own money. The VISTA teachers at the Rough Rock Demonstration School on the eroded terrain of Black Mesa, about 50 miles to the south have not had that problem. The school, funded by the B.I.A. and Office of Economic Opportunity, boards 360 boys and girls through seventh grade, and also has education courses for 300 adults. The program is a unique experiment in Navajo education—it is controlled by a Navajo school board, six of whose seven members never went to school.

Dr. Robert A. Roessel, the 41-year-old director, who is married to a Navajo, is the catalyst; he emphasizes what he calls the *both-and* approach.

The Indian is taught to be both Indian and American: proud of his heritage *and* learning to live successfully in modern America. The classrooms have the very latest of modern paraphernalia, including movable furniture, TV sets, the newest of textbooks; there are airy, modern dormitories and dining rooms. Traditional crafts and adornments of hogan life are also displayed. The staff of teachers is half white, half Navajo; singers (as medicine men are called) come in to record their chants and the legends and history of the tribe.

The school received five Vistas this year; two remain (one left to get married, one had problems at home, one simply couldn't take the isolation). In contrast, three Vistas from a previous group decided to stay on after their year's service to become part of the regular paid teaching staff.

Frank Setter, a tall, easy-going 24-year-old from a farm family in Crary, North Dakota (population 200), has been a Vista since 1966; he has a degree in social work. Frank asked to be assigned to this Indian reservation—he arrived this January—and he told me: "Vistas don't like to admit it, but we're getting much more out of VISTA than we're putting into it."

Frank lives in a trailer near the Black Mesa school. He has a twofold assignment: social work with retarded or disabled children and liaison work with families in the area to get to know their needs. The children love him, rough-house with him, hang about him in the gymnasium when he organizes a basketball game.

In a first-grade classroom of 27 children, from 7 to 12 years of age, Sandra (Sandy) Harrod quietly but firmly makes her presence felt as the children crowd around her at a table piled with new workbooks. The 23-year-old Skidmore College graduate, a composed blonde in a blue knit suit, has communication problems. She had no instruction in Navajo during her training period, though she is taking courses now. She finds the Navajo children different from the Anglos that she has taught: "I think this is the problem of the culturally deprived child, with whom I've had little experience. They crave attention—they're so eager for approval. They're constantly bringing papers to me with one answer written down, asking 'Is this right? . . . Is this one right?' Then they do the same with one more answer."

Sandy enjoys it here so much that she plans to go on the staff as a regular teacher when her VISTA term ends in August. Why? "Because of the challenge. But also because I think I'm afraid of the East Coast rut which I could sink into if I went back there."

In addition to education, the VISTA activity on the reservation includes these programs:

Health. At Lupton, a village of about 600 persons, most on welfare, Laurel Beggin has found a great deal of illness—mostly colds, pneumonia, trachoma, impetigo. The 22-year-old nurse from St. Paul, Minnesota, says the problem is not so much a fear of using white man's medicine but rather lack of transportation to medical centers. "The Indians often wait until they're quite sick before they get themselves into a hospital," she explains. Carolyn Domsic adds: "I have never seen so much illness that shoes and warm clothing alone could cure."

Crafts. At Naschitti, Gloria Leach (a hairdresser from West Haverstraw, New York) and Susanne Horton (a temporary dropout from American University in Washington, D.C.) encourage the Navajos to "do their own thing"—but to do it better. Gloria proudly displayed a spinning wheel made, with her encouragement, by a Navajo husband in the chapter; she has hopes that it can be electrified. Gloria has set up a "beauty shop" and she has a regular clientele of Navajo ladies who come for haircuts and sets. One day recently, a "customer," Mrs. Georgia Clani, showed the girls how to cut up a leg of mutton for stew. "This is OJT—on-the-job-training—for Vistas," said Mrs. Clani.

Nutrition. Most of the Vistas are involved in homemaking projects, encouraging a more balanced diet as part of a preventive medicine approach. Some of the girls have found that the Navajo women don't know how to use the commodity foods provided by state welfare—the cheese, oatmeal, dried peas and beans, tinned meat and rice. Some have given the meat to their dogs; others have fed the peas to their farm animals or simply thrown the food away. One day I watched Red Mesa Vistas in Mrs. Blackwater's kitchen show how to cook a rich stew of the tinned meat, peas and potatoes. "Delicious," agreed the Navajo ladies.

Agriculture. Vistas have shown the Indian men improved farming and irrigation techniques, including an experimental planting of hybrid crops. And Navajo children are being helped to raise their own calves in a 4-H club. When the calves were sold at auction, Susanne Horton says, parents learned that "proper feeding and watering of a calf brings in a lot more money for cattle." Children come to her meetings from distances as great as seven miles—a true sign of the Vista's success.

Community Development. This is a less tangible program: to inspire the Navajos to get over their deep-rooted apathy and initiate and take responsibility for projects. One technique VISTA uses was demonstrated at Pine Springs, where preschool classes were being held under makeshift conditions; the Vistas abruptly terminated the classes, announcing that they would not be resumed until the children had a proper schoolhouse. Months passed, but finally the Navajo men reacted; they have just completed building the first such schoolhouse in the chapter.

Yet despite such seeming successes, the VISTA program on the reservation here has had more than its share of failures. Winning the acceptance of the Indians has been a major stumbling block, sometimes aggravated by a legacy of hostility. The experience of the husband-wife team of Douglas and Edith Crow provides an example.

The newly married Crows are stationed at Indian Wells. He has a fine arts degree from Kansas City Art Institute; she is a Woodrow Wilson Fellow with a master's degree in English. They had been preceded at Indian Wells by another couple, with no VISTA connection—hippies types who had taught preschool children. They lived in a hogan and alienated the people with their unkempt appearance and phony efforts to be Indians. The Indians couldn't understand why Anglos wanted to desert their own culture. Chapter leaders complained to tribal headquarters and asked to be rid of them, and O.N.E.O. terminated their employment.

The Crows, an attractive young couple, are patiently waiting for the negative feelings to die away. They deliberately live like "squares" in a two-room frame house in the chapter compound, not in a hogan. Doug is even prepared to shave off his mustache, if the clean-shaven Navajos prefer him that way.

The chapter asked Doug tentatively to "make something," and he initiated a demonstration home-improvement project—he built a wall-length clothes closet with sliding doors in a large empty hogan used only for meetings and recreation programs. In the kitchen of her home Edith waits for the Navajo women to come so that she can show them how to vary their diet. "I don't go on home visits," Edith says, "because this community is very negative toward Anglos, owing to the past history. We feel that, in a sense, if we can bring their estimation back up to the zero point, we will have succeeded."

The Crows get few Navajo callers, but one man came by the house to ask, "Can we have a class in fractions and big words?"

"Yes," Doug replied eagerly. "When shall we begin?"

"Okay. Fine. I'll come by again in the evening."

The incident happened two weeks before my visit. The Crows were still waiting for him to come by.

The problem of acceptance plagues the VISTA program. For all their seeming dedication, many Vistas lack the maturity and insight necessary for the Navajo project. Though the former Indian Wells teachers were not Vistas, they typify many volunteers who have come here burdened by personal hang-ups. Among early teams were college dropouts with little training. Some considered themselves "saviors" of the Indians—they had ideas of revolutionizing life on the reservation. Some came out of bizarre, personal needs to be one with the Noble Savage. Some figured that VISTA was a sabbatical. Many were known to both tribe members and Anglos here as "the dirty beatnicks." (The Navajos were particularly puzzled by their bearded, unwashed appearance because for generations the white man has maintained that he is superior to the Indian in cleanliness and grooming.)

Last summer one group of Vistas often congregated in the Gallup (New Mexico) apartment of a VISTA field officer for parties and "recuperation." There were rumors that the "tea" was being smoked. The situation was sufficiently serious to bring VISTA's regional director in from San Francisco, and soon after the field officer left, the parties stopped.

When Tom Atcitty, the Navajo VISTA supervisor, was hired by

Washington VISTA 18 months ago, his people asked him cynically whether the volunteers were "being sent out here for *their* rehabilitation." The first thing Tom did was to lay down rules about clothes, the use of Government vehicles (some Vistas had taken to driving them down to Mexico) and manners generally.

Because of the strong, negative feelings of the Navajos in some areas, Tom has spent much of his time just repairing the emotional damage to his tribe, by visiting the chapters, having long talks with key Navajos and trying to restructure the projects to fit local needs. He still has problems with immature Vistas, and with the VISTA bureaucracy.

Certain Vistas here were selected, after a year's service, to be volunteer leaders to help orient new recruits, but these young people, apparently feeling that they are invested with a special power, tend to ignore Tom or policy. They take their orders from a VISTA program officer sitting miles away in Phoenix, Arizona, and from the area coordinator sitting in San Francisco. And although Tom Atcitty was hired by VISTA, is paid by VISTA on a grant to the O.N.E.O. here, he is often bypassed by the regional officials. The volunteer leaders, who have little knowledge of the Navajos, their language, their over-all needs and hopes, are periodically called to San Francisco for talks. "I'm their supervisor," Tom told me. "Yet I've never been called to those talks."

"Against this background," Tom adds bluntly, "I feel that just getting Vistas accepted by my people has been the *main* achievement really. We're getting the repercussions now from the earlier Vistas. Some of them were just placed here by Washington, by people thousands of miles away who knew practically nothing about the Navajo reservation. Even O.N.E.O. didn't know that certain volunteers were on the reservation. With this type of beginning, it's a wonder that we even have a VISTA program here. Now I think we're in position to get involved in projects that can produce something tangible."

There does seem to be growing support for the VISTA program on the reservation. Tom Shirley, the Navajo chapter president at Lupton, told me: "It's hard to pry the Navajos out of their traditional reluctance, but I think they're coming out now—with the help of the Vistas." At a special Red Mesa chapter meeting, called to consider community action, I heard a number of the 75 men and women praise the work of the VISTA team of Jo-Anne and Carolyn.

But the people at that meeting also expressed their views on other matters: the critical need for more industry on the reservation, for more jobs, for "experts with skills who can teach us welding and give us farm training," for a high school. They told bitterly of their jobless young men who leave the reservation, seeking work in St. Louis and Cleveland and Los Angeles. "Why do our boys have to leave," they asked, "when there is so much to be done here?"

The need for expert help was emphasized by Peter MacDonald, O.N.E.O.'s executive director. He told me that last year there were 80 Vistas here; the number dwindled to 15 six months ago, and now there are 36. "The Vistas—many of them—have made a tremendous contribution, just by being here and taking on one or two specific community projects," he said. "But the reason that recruiting has not kept pace with our need is because the people also want more *quality* volunteers—people with vocational skills who can contribute to the effort to become self-sufficient; people with engineering background; people with knowledge in agriculture and range management and water development."

One hopeful development has been the recent decision in Washington to concentrate training of the Navy's Construction Battalion reservists—the Seabees—on the reservation. Last summer, the Seabees completed a pilot project at Red Rock, south of Gallup, preparing a school site, wiring an arts building, repairing the only bridge to the community. Now "Operation Navajo" is planned to take effect in August, 1969—a major, continuing training operation involving 7,000 Seabees that will result in better roads, dams, bridges. The Navajos will be hired to work side by side with the Seabees.

The program is particularly pleasing to the tribe and VISTA because it was inspired by Mrs. Margaret Sell, a Vista whose work was so admired by the Navajos that they asked her to join the paid staff at tribal headquarters. It was she who first suggested the Seabee project to the Navy.

Just before my trip to the reservation, I talked in Washington with William H. Crook, then director of VISTA, a 43-year-old veteran of many Presidential assignments involving volunteers and refugees. (He has since been appointed Ambassador to Australia.) Mr. Crook described the life of the VISTA volunteer with grim humor: "People *want* to be expendable. People don't want to be coddled. We send out VISTA volunteers into danger, and we neglect them. Their checks are late. They're trained for one job and are apt to be sent to another. All they get out of it is a 32-cent pin at the end of their year's service and their stipend, and a certificate perhaps with their name misspelled."

There are, as I discovered, other urgent problems faced by the Vistas on the reservation here; yet, as many of them told me, the human rewards—though often intangible—are worth all their efforts and sacrifices. The essential element in this equation is the nature of the individual volunteer.

He (or she) must be a mature, practical, sensitive person, capable of great human insight. He needs longer, more intensive training before entering this basically "foreign" nation, training in the language and the culture of the people he seeks to motivate and to help. He must have special skills and experience to offer toward the creation of a labor pool that will attract industry and create jobs—for the Indians want passionately to be done with handouts and paternalism and to become self-supporting.

Only with such people as these can the VISTA program on the Navajo reservation really fulfill its great promise.

> The Pueblo Indians have been in contact with people of European descent for four centuries. During this time, they engaged in armed warfare with the Spaniards, yet ended by accepting Catholicism and Spanish dominion. Before the time of the Spaniards, and during and after it, the Pueblos were also engaged in armed conflict with other Indian peoples, such as the Apache. Despite the pressures of predatory Indians and whites, the Pueblos have continued to endure.
>
> For most non-Indian observers, endurance as a people must

imply the absence of change, but this is inaccurate, for peoples who refuse to change at all become extinct. The peoples who have endured as recognized and organized entities have been sufficiently flexible to change just enough to maintain themselves in their environments. The Taos adopted Catholicism but they have also maintained native religious and ceremonial practices; exactly how they are integrated, outsiders are not sure, but for the Taos Indians there is no difficulty. The contradiction is in the mind of the rational observer who insists upon a consistency based upon his view of the situation.

Have other Americans lost their identity as American because unlike their ancestors they neither live in log cabins, make their own soap, nor apprentice their children at adolescence? Have Frenchmen lost their identity as French because they work in factories rather than on peasant farms and consume soft drinks in addition to wine? For the peoples involved, these kinds of changes are serious and become the topic for heated political and moral arguments. Some Americans are sure that the vigor of their people was sapped when their children ceased to be members of the labor force and instead were required to attend school until age sixteen or later. Some Taos Indians see the fiber of their people as being eroded by the adoption of motor cars and household electricity. An observer would be rash who in either case predicted the downfall of the community or nation from the acceptance of a novel trait. "Generation gaps" are usually a sign of communal health; it is conformity that is a sign of stagnation and decay.

The Taos Indians Have a Small Generation Gap. Winthrop Griffith | In summer, the warm wind rushes over the mesas and up the sloping plains from the southwest. It

SOURCE: *New York Times*, February 21, 1971.

picks up speed at the foot of the Taos Mountains to swirl dust across the big open area in the middle of the pueblo nestled there. Tourists come by the thousands daily to gaze at the five-tiered, adobe mud buildings which still seem a part of the earth. Their cars jam the dusty plaza and the two miles of roadway leading in from the main highway, and the air is filled with impatient noises.

Now, the plaza is a bit muddy and almost empty. A chilly breeze comes gently out of the broad canyon rising to the east. A few old men stand silently next to the pueblo's walls, occasionally adjusting the thin blankets which cover their heads. Several children skid and play on shelves of ice which fringe the river flowing down the mountains from the Blue Lake and running through the middle of the plaza. The sounds are few and nice: laughter from the children, a rustle of the breeze in the surrounding grove of cottonwoods, the rush of river water over the rocks and between the ice.

Early winter is "Quiet Season" in the Taos Pueblo, a time which ancient custom and the orders of the Pueblo Council reserve "to let the earth rest." The younger men who work in the town three miles south ignored the ban against driving cars, and the children in the school at the edge of the pueblo were engaged in the happy bedlam of producing a musical play when I came here. But most of the 1,400 Taos Indians walked softly and spoke in near whispers.

"Quiet Season" inhibited any overt celebration of one of the great victories in the thousand-year history of the tribe: Congressional action which returned control of 48,000 acres of mountain lands east of the pueblo and surrounding Blue Lake, which the Indians worship as a sacred source of life.

On the day in December when the United States Senate completed Congressional action to end a 64-year legislative battle by the Taos Indians, the bell of the Church of San Geronimo in the pueblo rang, but that was the only sound of celebration. I was here the day President Nixon signed the act into law. Even the church bell was silent then, and only one old man stood in the plaza.

I told him the news from the radio, and he nodded in understanding.

He muttered a few words in Tiwa, the breathy, slightly clipped Taos language, then tried to tell me in bits of English and Spanish what the victory meant: "The water in this river here comes from Blue Lake. Our ancestors came out of Blue Lake, long ago. Blue Lake nourishes everything. It is the source of our wisdom, of our life . . . Do you understand?"

I didn't, but I was moved by the tear which swelled slowly out of his eye. It curved around his broad, shallow nose, moved faster in a deep wrinkle of his dark skin and then formed again, on his chin before dropping off into the mud. He made no embarrassed motion to brush the tear away as I watched it. "I am very, very happy," he said quietly.

The Taos Pueblo is unique, even among the score of other pueblos (the word is Spanish, meaning town) in New Mexico. The people of all of them revere the earth and formally worship the "shrines" (a stream, a grove of trees, a meadow) on it. Taos, farther north and east than any of the villages, more toughly resists the influences and pressures of modern America than any of them.

Some sociologists consider Taos the most "backward" of all the pueblos. The council of 40 older men who rule it do not allow electricity or other modern conveniences in the main pueblo buildings, and there is no democratic vote—as in all other pueblos—to choose the leaders.

A few anthropologists understand that the Taos Indians are more religiously dependent on the sacred shrines of the land than any other group or tribe. Dr. John J. Bodine, a young anthropology teacher at American University in Washington who lived with or close to the Taos Pueblo as he grew up, said without qualification in Congressional testimony: "If Blue Lake and the surrounding lands are not returned to the tribe it will effectively destroy Taos culture."

That ancient culture is rooted deeply and religiously in the earth. No other group of Americans has clung so tenaciously to customs which relate and link—in the words of one Taos leader—"the human soul and the earth."

It's hard to see at first. To an outsider's eye, paradoxes abound:

· The Taos Indians belligerently complain that non-Indian hunters and campers littered the shores of Blue Lake with empty bean cans and other ugly things. But I could see discarded soft-drink cans and candy wrappers at the edges of the river running through the plaza, and other metallic and paper debris littering several spots in the pueblo.

· The elders on the council boast that they are keeping their community "pure and uncorrupted by television and plumbing." But they have reluctantly caved in to the demands of their younger brothers in recent years to allow generators, wells and other man-made conveniences in the homes around the periphery of the pueblo.

· Each year, most of the boys around age 10 in the Taos Pueblo are removed from their families and the schools to spend 18 months in secret religious training in ceremonial chambers called "kivas" dug underground many centuries ago. But several teenage boys I talked with wore bell-bottom trousers and stylishly striped shirts, and they aspired to ownership of Pontiac Firebird cars and "to get way from here" some day.

· The ancient religious ceremonies, dances and prayers of the Taos Indians—the details of more of them are kept secret from outsiders—seem to be intensely felt and emotionally genuine. But 90 per cent of the people here are also Catholic.

I challenged Frank Marcus, a 40-year-old Taos leader, on some of the apparent conflicts.

He's a rancher, living in one of the few homes at the edge of the pueblo that has a generator, television and manufactured furniture. On the wall over one bed in the big room in which we talked, I could see a small, framed photograph of Blue Lake and also a stark, wood cross.

"No other people I know have this relationship between mother earth and the soul," Marcus said.

"Yes, most of us are Catholic. But that is not in conflict with our older Indian religion. We worship life—the water, the trees, all the growing things. We could make room for a newborn child who came into the world to teach us. We regard every man as an individual brother.

"Blue Lake is our ultimate shrine, the source of life for birds, trees, everything. But there are shrines everywhere in those 48,000 acres. We do not build any structures by them. If I were to build a structure by a shrine, there would not be a shrine anymore. A Catholic priest would not worship at a torn-down shrine.

"Our forefathers said that someday the white man would understand. The land and everything living on it has human meaning to us. It must remain natural and wild. . . .

"The United States is beginning to understand. At least you are worrying about what you call 'ecology.' This is something simple and true which we have known for thousands of years."

Little is known about the religious ceremonies which the Taos Indians conduct in their underground kiva chambers or at the shrines high in the Sangre de Cristo Mountains around Blue Lake. The worship and the prayers are offered in strict privacy, often with guards posted at the kiva entrances or on the trails leading to the shrines. Even the most trusted non-Indians, men who have lived in and studied the pueblo for decades, are kept away from the religious ceremonies.

The reasons for the extreme secrecy are both mystical and pragmatic. Marcus and other pueblo leaders say only that the presence of non-Indians would somehow "interrupt" the sanctity of the ceremonies and the shrines and that any man-made structures "desecrate" the sacred grounds. A history of Spanish oppression and religious persecution also forced many Taos ceremonies, literally, to go underground.

None of the members of the tribe itself know all the details of the religious rituals, not even the 90-year-old cacique who is the spiritual leader of the pueblo. Anthropologist Bodine told a puzzled Congressional committee:

"Taos religion is like a mosaic composed of bits and pieces of knowledge with each part known only to a restricted number of individuals. If an individual's religious duties are not properly performed and transmitted to his successor, which is done in absolute secrecy, then the religion cannot function . . . Outsiders constitute a great threat to the proper performance of those duties; their very presence is contaminating. It constitutes a serious invasion of religious privacy, and, as the Taos have explained, any alteration or destruction of the ecology of the area has the potential of eliminating properties of the environment that are crucial to correct ritual performance—for example, only certain plants can be used in specific rituals."

Paul Bernal, the politically powerful secretary to the Pueblo Council, confirms the Taos determination for religious privacy, but speaks more poetically of what it's all about.

"That land—the 48,000 acres which we now control—is our church and our school. It is filled with life, given by God. God makes a determination of what you will be even before you are a human being. And that's the way it is with the evergreens—a fir, or an aspen or some other pine— and with the animals up there—the deer and elk, blue grouse and squirrels, the black bear and wild turkey.

"All these are like people; we do not discriminate about life, in our prayers and action.

"I am sorry but we cannot let other people in, non-Indians. I have seen what the United States Government does to the land, with its so-called multiple-use policy for conservation, commercial development and recreation. It is desecrated, ruined. We will conduct a survey of all 48,000 acres, train some of our own people in forest management and then fence it all. We'll use natural materials for the fence, fallen timbers, to keep the land private and sacred.

"The new law prohibits us from any commercial gain from the land. That is fine with us. We will hunt a bit on it, taking only what is necessary. We are responsible, really, for the shelter of all the wildlife. That's the reason we don't believe in cutting the trees. We are responsible to help let nature take its own course, to follow its own purposes. We must let the place be fertile.

"We are trying to make this place as holy as possible. . . ."

In 1906, the United States Government seized the 48,000 acres and much more in which the Taos Indians had hunted and worshiped for centuries. By executive order, President Theodore Roosevelt placed Blue Lake and 130,000 acres of Taos Territory into Carson National Forest and under the jurisdiction of the United States Forest Service.

For decades, the Indians were confused. Few of them understood English in the early part of the century. They knew only that their land was being desecrated by wire fences, timber cutting and recreation trails which brought non-Indian hunters and campers in to tramp on their shrines.

The Taos Indians learned English. They learned about land-title documents, lobbying in Congress, raising money from rich old ladies to pay for trips to Washington, and the phrases of justice which appealed to a nation and Congress aware of guilt.

They compromised, giving up 82,000 of the acres which the Indian Claims Commission ruled in 1965 had been unjustly taken by the Government. They refused money offered by the Government and persistently pursued the goal of ownership of Blue Lake and the essential 48,000 acres.

In recent years, the House of Representatives twice approved legislation giving the Taos Pueblo title to the 48,000 acres, to be held in trust by the Interior Department. (This is standard procedure for Indian reservation lands throughout the nation, and was acceptable to the Taos Indians.) The Senate balked at first, concerned about the precedent of returning a large bloc of land because of the Indian Claims Commission estimate that 90 per cent of the continental United States could be claimed by various tribes through "aboriginal title." But in December, with the support of President Nixon and the leadership of Senator Fred Harris of Oklahoma, the Senate voted 70 to 12 for the House bill.

Some non-Indian people of the area are critical of the Congressional action, skeptical of Indian motives and uncomprehending of the religious meaning of it all. "Okay, so they worship at Blue Lake," said one cattleman worried about his grazing rights. "But 48,000 acres? That's one hell of a big church." Some local Forest Service officials are dubious about the future care of the Blue Lake watershed and bureaucratically irritated that so much land has been taken out of their jurisdiction. (Carson National Forest should survive; it still contains 1,177,408 acres of northern New Mexico lands.)

They are in for some rough negotiations with pueblo leaders to work out details of the change-over. Bernal notes that the Federal Government is still responsible for fire-prevention measures on the lands and wants to use bulldozers to build fire-trails. He spat out the word "bulldozers" in contempt, and broke out of his whispery voice to shout "Never!"

Few of the Indians live up in the high, rugged lands which they have just won. They've had exclusive use of portions of it for years, but have gone into it only for religious ceremonies or hunting. Sustained human survival would be tough in the steep canyons and on the high peaks of the Taos and Sangre de Cristo ranges; much of the land is above 10,000 feet.

The people prefer, as their ancestors have since at least the eighth century, to remain within the closely knit community of the pueblo itself, at the 7,000-foot level. It's a beautiful spot, at the base of the blue-green bulk of Pueblo Peak rising sharply to 12,300 feet. Level grassland, dotted with cattle, horses and even a few buffaloes, stretches away in the other direction toward distant desert horizons. Close around the pueblo itself are cornfields, a few apple orchards, some clusters of wild plum trees and a circle of roughly constructed corrals for the livestock. In the clean winter air, the smells are sweet: from new stacks of hay, from freshly cut pine planks on one fence, from pinon logs burning in ovens inside the pueblo dwellings.

The land, the religion wrapped around it and the adobe pueblo buildings rising out of it have changed little since Spanish explorers found Taos in the 1500's and recorded their descriptions. Glass or screens cover the small windows of the main dwellings, metal vent pipes poke through the roofs and the women use aluminum buckets to pull water from the river. But those are the only accommodations to modern convenience and comfort visible from the plaza.

The central area of the pueblo remains unchanged because of both the conservatism of the council of old men who run it and the streak of commercialism in the community during the summer tourist time. "It's historic, unique and a drawing card," acknowledges Tony Reyna, who operates the only thriving Indian crafts shop nearby. Parking and photography fees ($1 each) are the only sources of revenue for the pueblo as a whole; the several hundred thousands of dollars raised each year are spent on general improvements, salaries for pueblo leaders and attorney fees for such battles as the Blue Lake legislative effort.

Change—and tensions between the ancient and the modern—is more apparent in the newly built-up areas at the periphery of the pueblo and in the attitudes and customs of the younger Indians.

The generators, water wells and even propane gas tanks in the homes at the edges of the pueblo are allowed as a result of concessions wrested from the tradition-fixed elders. ("We can keep our heritage while enjoying some of the modern comforts," a young man said in paraphrasing his argument for me. "We have to stay pure and close to the earth," responds an old man. "Plumbing and television are corrupting. The 'Beverly Hillbillies' can do nothing for us.")

The Taos Indians are also shedding the customs of 300 years of Spanish influence. The older men have such names as "Jesus" and "Quirino," and they speak Spanish as the second language. The given names of almost all the children are now Anglo, and most of the adults under age 40 speak English with little conflicting accent. But beneath the changes of outside cultural influences, all remain Indian. Among themselves and most naturally, they use the unwritten Tiwa language, and everybody in the pueblo retains an Indian name which honors the earth and its natural life.

In essence, the Taos Pueblo seems to cling rigidly to those ancient customs which it considers important and to discard or adopt—with subtle discrimination—parts of the surrounding cultures.

The surface changes are most obvious in the school and the children in it. It is financed by the Bureau of Indian Affairs and is situated at the southern edge of the pueblo area, in a fenced compound of several Government-owned buildings in the shadow of a high, ugly water-tank tower. (The Government doesn't trust the water from Blue Lake; some tests indicate possible pollution in the river from which the Indians drink, though a local physician reports there are only a few cases of mild diarrhea, during the summer.)

On the walls of the earlier grades, there are the simple, charming sketches and paintings typical of children anywhere: trees and flowers, airplanes and houses with smoky chimneys, and one stick figure in a starkly triangular dress, with the caption "This Is Me. Who Am I?" The first-grade classroom was adorned with 20-word compositions, structured by the teacher as letters to Santa Claus. The names of the authors were Anglo-Saxon: Kevin, Karen, Bobby S. and Shirley. Most of the boys wanted a BB gun; almost all of the girls asked for a Barbie Doll.

There are no apparent resentments by the people of the pueblo that their children are attending a conventional white man's school. The parents or grandparents take care of the private cultural and religious education, and then there is the secret kiva training for 18 months. ("They come back from that with their hair long and with a deep sort of maturity," says principal Larry Labrum.) But like parents anywhere, they are eager for their children to learn how to read, write and do math.

The school offers some knowledge about Indians in America and even some details of particular tribes and nations; but with full approval and even demand by the Pueblo Council, its teachers steer clear of any education in Taos culture.

With a few qualifications, the Indians consider the school their own. They built it, with W.P.A. funds, during the Depression. The school board, which shares policy and administrative authority with the B.I.A principal, is all Indian. Although the B.I.A. bans corporal punishment, the parents and the Indian school board have repeatedly told the staff to "swat them good" if any of the children become discipline-defiant.

The rub and the resentment is in the make-up of the staff. All of the custodial and kitchen personnel and the 10 paid teachers' aides are out of the pueblo, but seven of the 10 teachers are non-Indian. Teaching positions at the school remain under the rigid regulations of Civil Service, and the school board is currently fighting that flaw in the school with the B.I.A. and Washington.

That squabble isn't really tearing the place apart, however. Almost 200 of the pueblo's children attend the B.I.A school, but parents of another 100 send them to the public school in the town three miles south. They have a choice between the two schools, which seems to be made in part on the basis of a desire for earlier integration with Anglo and Spanish-American children and in part on how close they live to the bus stop for the public school pickup. The kids have to walk to the B.I.A. school just south of the pueblo, and for some it's a long, cold walk in the winter.

Most of the Taos children go on to the junior high school and then complete high school in the town, and about 15 per cent of them continue with college or advanced vocational training. The staff of the pueblo school, both Indian and non-Indian, is reluctant to generalize and is supersensitive to any suggested or imagined stereotyping. But they report that the Taos children are extraordinarily talented in language, particularly and naturally skilled in art, and often brilliant in dancing and poetry.

Julie Westphal, the young kindergarten teacher, also suggests another distinguishing characteristic of the Taos children: "In general, the kids are not competitive. In our society, the kids pick up the idea that they gotta get that 'A,' before Johnny does. Here, the kids don't really care about that. The more they are pushed by the teachers—in a competitive sense—the more they withdraw."

Tony Reyna, the proprietor of the one thriving arts and crafts shop and the chairman of the school board, is impatient with his people's lack of competitiveness economically. He opened up about what he called the "too peaceful, too satisfied" attitudes of his people.

Reyna himself may not be exactly the model of an aggressively profit-seeking businessman, despite the success of his store and his current role as president of the Kiwanis Club in town. Prominently displayed on the front counter of his shop is an admonishing sign: "RUSHING MAY BE YOUR THING—WE DON'T CATER TO HASTY BUYERS." He proudly pointed out to me a large bowl of marvelously simple lines and grainy texture, which he refused to sell two years ago to a lady who thumped a $100 bill on his counter and announced she would use it as a bird-bath in her patio. "That's a very old, very beautiful Indian-made thing," Reyna said with lingering anger. "I won't sell it to anybody who won't appreciate it."

He is irritated personally that most of the items in his shop are made by other tribes and that the Taos Pueblo isn't capitalizing enough on the tourist trade.

"There's no real need for our people to go away to work. The potential is so great here, with all the tourists, that all of our people could make a darn good living by converting from farmers to craft people. They could establish factories, retail and wholesale outlets for moccasins, drums.

"We have all the materials right here, on our lands, and we have the time. . . .

"Most of the people here are happy and have enough to eat; our lands and farms produce enough food. But we are really a poor pueblo compared to some others. The trouble is we're too peaceful and satisfied, and don't have enough incentive. We could do so much better."

Reyna remains one of the few businessmen in the pueblo, despite his continuing efforts to talk others into joining together for commercial purposes. Most of the people continue in small-scale farming as they have for centuries, raising enough for their own needs but not enough to compete with corporate food wholesalers and chain grocery stores.

And there aren't enough jobs in the area for those who do not farm. About 300 of them work for wages in the town of Taos, at a lumber mill or in the innumerable art galleries and service firms catering to tourists. The Anglo and Spanish-American employers are eager to hire Taos Indians ("They're hard, no-nonsense workers," said one), but unemployment remains high for all in the area, about 12 per cent.

An estimated 400 have left the pueblo and the area for better opportunities in Albuquerque, Denver and other scattered spots in the nation. The small number of them with advanced education are professionally successful in the cities, but most of them struggle painfully at low wages in an alien white world and almost all of those who do leave eventually return to Taos.

"I tried it for eight years," said one man who is now back tending a small herd of cattle and a few acres of cornfields. "I made about $85 a week in Los Angeles. But the rent for a shack was $100 a month, and there were bills for electric lights and other things. I liked to take a bus along Wilshire Boulevard sometimes to see all the new white buildings. But I could never breathe deeply there, and I didn't want to die there."

When the temporary visitor hears the people of the Taos Pueblo talk that way in a setting of natural beauty and apparent peace, there's a temptation for him to romanticize the place. But the routine life of many of the Indians is incomplete or even tragic. As in any community, there are ugly blemishes in the Taos Pueblo.

Dr. James Dorman, assigned to the United States Public Health Service clinic near the school, is impressed by the basic physical hardiness of the Indians. "Tuberculosis is unusual, arterial heart disease is rare, and

I've seen no cancer cases this year," he reported. "They don't seem to die of anything; they just get to be 90 or 100 years old and then fade away."

"But there's something else," he said sadly. "Alcoholism is rampant. There is a father or grandfather who is a chronic alcoholic in many if not most of the families. Violence is increasing. I have to treat stab wounds often in the clinic, and there have been two or three murders—at least— in the past few years."

Why?

"I don't know," he answered. "Most of them seem happy emotionally and they are tough and resilient physically. One old lady—she's 102 years old—has been in here three times this past year. She should, by clinical standards, have died each time, but she didn't and she left cheerful each time. But for others, younger ones mainly, there's some deep need unfulfilled. Maybe it's despair."

Late one night, I stood with three young Taos men for an hour in utter darkness and near silence. They had been standing for several hours earlier against the wall of the single grocery store of the pueblo, at the corner of the only intersection of roadway and alley needing a stop sign. Near midnight, there were no cars at all, nothing to watch.

One of them wore stylishly mod clothes. I was aware in the dim, dim starlight that he was about 18 years old. He said nothing. He held a push-button knife, and kept clicking it in the dark.

The second boy spoke just once during the hour. "What are you doing here, man? You don't belong here." Then somehow he understood what I was up to and lapsed into accepting silence.

The third boy told me he was 15. He was more curious and expressive than his two friends. Waiting for nothing at the intersection, he broke through the silence, about once every 10 minutes:

"What is your name? Where are you from? . . .

"What's it like in the city, in Los Angeles, San Francisco and New York, where you have been? Did you like it? Were you afraid? Did you have enough to eat? . . .

"We stay here because it is our home, that's all. We are close to something here. I don't know how to tell you what it is. But we belong. If I were a poet, maybe I could tell you. See those stars there? Feel that breeze on your face? Hear the river out there? I suppose that's why we stay. . . .

"The trouble is that we wonder what it's like out there. We get bored sometimes, and there's a sort of loneliness."

In the daytime, there's much less introspective questioning and a definitely pleasant mood in the pueblo. For all their religious secrecy and their disdain of sociological inquiry, the Taos Indians easily smile, eagerly offer friendly waves and invariably call out a warm "Hi" as they pass a visitor. Extremely close relationships can develop for someone who stays longer. Julie Westphal was literally taken into the family of Jimmie and Rose Cordova a few months after her arrival. She now naturally addresses Mrs. Cordova as "Mom" and an older daughter as "Sis."

The people of the pueblo are amused by the Indian stereotypes sustained by most white Americans, and rightly so. They are not at all "sullen" or "humorless." One man said, with a tone of infinite and melodramatic respect just after meeting me: "The Sunday New York Times? That's a fine newspaper. I got a copy once, and it kept us in kindling for a month." A young Taos woman with hair to her waist said as she rinsed some clothes in the river: "No, I'm not really living here. I'm just a hippie trying to find Truth."

Apocryphal or not, I liked the story of how an old man handled a tourist last summer who kept asking insulting questions about whether or not it was "safe" to touch what he presumed to be the germ-laden items in the curio shop. The old man placed his face and breath about two inches away from the tourist's nose and said calmly: "It's okay. I've had a virulent, highly contagious form of hepatitis for two years, and I'm still alive."

They also like to poke fun at anthropologists who descend on them in the summer, at Bureau of Indian Affairs' personnel shakeups ordered from Washington and—sometimes—at themselves.

I found few hints of Third World awareness and no sweeping denunciations of Western, white, technological, oppressive society—such as those from militant young black Americans and an increasing number of Indians of other tribes. The Taos Indians are angrily conscious of past and recent injustices by an oppressive or patronizing Government. ("I'd rather negotiate with the Chinese Communists," one Forest Service official remarked about their tenacity in fighting for their rights.) But they are not self-consciously consumed with antagonism toward the big and little symbols of the white society which surrounds them.

There was no indication of what we would call an "identity crisis" among the people of the pueblo. Unlike many tribes, Taos has a low incidence of suicide. The loneliness is present, yes, and so are other blemishes on the face of the serene life here. But the Taos Indians seem to know, deeply and simply, who they are and where their roots reach. They walk very comfortably on this land, which is now a sanctuary.

It may be a small sign, but I thought it was significant that all of the individuals I met kept their eyes riveted on mine, with none of the anxious evasions of most people in contact with inquisitive strangers. And I became aware during the days here that the mood of the place is free of fear, the kind of fear which pervades most cities and many towns in the nation today.

One man, who had returned to Taos after 12 years in the fragile cities of the West Coast, said with quiet pride, "We are a community. Maybe if any community can survive in this impatient world, we can. Perhaps we will last on again for as long as we have lasted, for a thousand years.

"That's a long time, and pretty good these days."

VI

PAN-INDIAN MILITANCY:
Indian Life
Is Indian Business

Since colonial times, there have been a series of movements among the various tribes toward establishing a common identity as Indians. Such movements are known as *pan-Indianism*, and they have manifested themselves in a variety of contexts: political, religious, and fraternal. On the political level, the problem is similar to that of organizing a league or union of the nations of the world: how to create and maintain an association that will express and develop the common interests of nations and peoples whose initial orientation is in terms of their own particular interests, fears, needs, and anxieties. So various are the Indian peoples and so disparate are their situations that allying them together in one association poses a major political problem.

In the United States, since the end of the Second World War, a score of associations have emerged trying to represent the Indians. Some associations recruit the memberships of individual Indians, others of tribes or local clubs, still others of tribal officers, and still others of combinations of the foregoing. Among these associations, the National Congress of American Indians (NCAI) is the oldest, the best established, and has the largest tribal membership. Even it operates under severe handicaps, because most tribes are poor and also need to be convinced that the NCAI can actually assist them in the handling of their own particular problems. Accordingly, the NCAI has found it difficult to enlist the membership of all organized Indian tribal units and to insist upon the full and prompt payment of dues. On several occasions, the NCAI has been on the verge of bankruptcy and dissolution, only to be rescued by the dedication of executive secretaries such as Vine Deloria, Jr., who held office 1964–67.

Deloria comes from a family well known in Siouan affairs: his father has been an eminent official of the Episcopalian Church; his aunt, Ella Deloria, devoted much of her life to linguistic and ethnographic researches. He himself trained for the ministry and then for the legal profession. In the essays reproduced here, he adopts alternately the postures of a Sioux and of a pan-Indian. From the latter posture, he outlines much of recent Indian history, from confinement on the reservations, the Dawes (General Allotment) Act of 1887, the Indian Reorganization Act of 1934, to the Nixon Administration of Indian Affairs. He is especially acute in explicating the terribly destructive effect on Indian communities of the application of Anglo-Saxon systems of heirship and welfare. Thereby the agents and agencies of the government approach Indian communities as if they were aggregates of individuals rather than members of an organic body. So, in the government view, Indian land became not tribal property over which sovereignty was sustained by an organized Indian people, but instead something to be divided and allotted to individual owners. As Deloria aptly remarks: how would it be possible for General Motors to conduct its corporate affairs, if the government were to insist on dealing directly with each of the GM shareholders and employes and were to regard the factories and machinery of the corporation as assets which could be sold at any moment and the proceeds divided per capita?

At the time they were written, both Deloria essays had a topical theme: in the one case, the Indian occupation of Alcatraz Island; in the other case, the Indian mistrust of Nixon policy in Indian affairs, as exemplified by his appointment of Walter Hickel as Secretary of the Interior. Both topics are now history, for after several years of occupation, the Indians have left or been removed from Alcatraz Island, and after some months as secretary, Hickel was asked to resign. Neither situation developed quite as observers might have anticipated. In the case of Alcatraz, there was considerable initial publicity, and numerous young and restless Indians came to visit and participate; yet the occupation failed to achieve anything concrete, except for the publicity and the example. Deloria hoped that the occupiers would remodel the prison facilities abandoned by the government and so transform the island into an Indian community. From his multifold experiences with Indian peoples, he should have known better. The militants who occupied Alcatraz shared anger and poverty in common, but lacked organization and common purpose, so that the site deteriorated rather than improved under the stresses of their occupancy. Had the NCAI or another national pan-Indian association with as dedicated an administrator as Deloria been in a position to guide and encourage the efforts of the occupants, and had such an administrator been able to merge these efforts with the funds and influences of benevolent foundations, then something positive—even great—might have issued from the Alcatraz occupation. Unhappily, the occupiers had neither disciplined organization nor clear goals, except to maintain themselves under conditions of poverty and adversity.

In the case of Walter Hickel, the forecasts were again in error. The hostility to Indian interests was centered elsewhere within the Nixon Administration. Under Hickel's leadership as Secretary of the Interior, some significant steps were taken toward extending the powers and responsibilities of tribal governments at the expense of the Bureau of Indian Affairs and the federal government. While the documents are not available for an assessment of his role in Indian affairs, his record appears much better than had been prophesied.

Regardless of the original inspirations and the topicality of these essays, the problems outlined by Vine Deloria, Jr., remain before the Indian and non-Indian citizens of the United States. Indian rights stated in treaties and laws and explicated in court decisions are still not being adequately protected by federal agencies. Governmental procedures continue to emphasize the rights of individual Indians at the expense of the solidarity of their communities and tribes. As individuals, Indians are relocating, and being relocated, into urban areas, where too many of them experience unemployment, poverty, and isolation, and so end in drunkenness and other pathologies. Outraged by these conditions Indians are moved to protest by flamboyant actions that follow the example of the seizure of Alcatraz Island, and decent men like Vine Deloria, Jr., try to explain to us what is going wrong and to guide us toward better conduct.

The War between the Redskins and the Feds. Vine Deloria, Jr. | If Secretary of the Interior Walter Hickel has any sense of history, he must have been impressed with his situation at the convention of the National Congress of American Indians held earlier this fall in Albuquerque, New Mexico. Not since George Armstrong Custer's sensitivity-training session on the banks of the Little Big Horn had so many angry Indians surrounded a representative of the United States Government with blood in their eyes. Of the estimated million Indians in the United States, the N.C.A.I. represents the reservation population of some 400,000. With spokesmen

Source: *New York Times*, December 7, 1969.

for the remaining urban and other Indian communities of the East (500,000 urban Indians and 100,000 scattered Eastern bands) attending the convention, Hickel was greeted by representatives of the entire Indian community, including Eskimos, Indians and Aleuts from his home state of Alaska.

All summer, tension had been building within the Indian community as the tribes fearfully awaited the pronouncement of Indian policy by the new Nixon Administration. During the 1968 Presidential campaign Nixon had promised that, if elected, he would not unilaterally sever Federal relations with the tribes, nor would he allow the tribes to be pressured to alter the relationship themselves. Indian leadership, recalling that Nixon had been Vice President during the Eisenhower Administration, when the hated policy of termination of Federal responsibilities for Indians had been forced on the unwary tribes, was alerted for any signs of change, and skeptical of the "New Federalism."

Hickel's performance in 1969 appeared to have justified Indian suspicions. In late July, at a Western Governors' Conference in Seattle, he characterized the relationship of the Federal Government as "overprotective" of Indian rights. With a foot-in-mouth aplomb so characteristic of some of Nixon's interchangeable Cabinet members, Hickel compounded this error by labeling the reservations as "crutches" by which Indians avoided their full responsibilities as citizens.

By late summer, the moccasin telegraph was buzzing with rumors that the new Secretary of the Interior was a "terminationist," and that a great battle over the very existence of the reservations was imminent. Indian reservations have a total land base of more than 52 billion acres, scattered in 26 states and providing a home for people of 315 different tribal groups. The life expectancy of a reservation Indian is 46 years, rising nearly a year each year under current programs. Although the average income is slightly over $1,500 per family annually, and the housing is generally substandard, the reservations are all that remain of the continent the Indians once owned, and they are determined to fight for every handful of dust that remains.

The National Traditionalist Movement, spearheaded by the Iroquois League, called for Hickel's removal from office. The Iroquois (the only Indian tribe to declare war on Germany in 1917) set a strong nationalistic tone to the resistance, which quickly sprang up in Indian country.

From the urban Indian centers on the West Coast, the third-world-oriented United Native Americans took up the battle cry. "IMPEACH HICKEL" bumper stickers blossomed beside "Red Power" and the multitude of "Custer" slogans on Indian cars. Petitions calling for Hickel's removal began to circulate on the coast.

As the N.C.A.I. convention opened, there was considerable discussion by the delegates as to the length at which Indians should *stabilize* Hickel's hairline. This remark was an obvious reference to Hickel's conception of his role as trustee in defending the water rights of the Pyramid Lake Paiutes of Nevada. The Pyramid Lake tribe has a beautiful lake, the largest fresh-water lake in the state. For the major part of this century it has tried to insure that sufficient water is delivered to the lake to maintain its excellent cutthroat trout fishery and its flock of pelicans. But the Federal Government has continually refused to defend the tribe's water rights by allowing other users to take water which is rightfully owned by the Paiutes. Consequently, the lake has had a declining shoreline for most of the century, a condition that precludes development of the reservation for recreation purposes.

Hickel's solution, proposed after a meeting with Governors Reagan of California and Laxalt of Nevada, was to reduce the water level 152 feet, creating a mud flat of 40,000 acres and thus "stabilizing" the water level. It was the same logic used by the Army to destroy a Vietnamese village—"We had to destroy the village to save it." It naturally followed that the only way to save Pyramid Lake was to drain it.

With these remarks to his credit, it is a wonder that Hickel was the recipient of only sporadic boos and catcalls when he attempted to address the Indian convention. No one even speculated on the possibility of a canine ancestor in Hickel's immediate family tree. "Terminationist" is a much dirtier word in the Indian vocabulary.

Wally Hickel is not that bad a guy. He was genuinely puzzled by the reactions which his remarks had created in the Indian community. In his own mind he was simply searching for a new approach to a problem that he, as Secretary of the Interior, had a responsibility to resolve. But he had unexpectedly hit the one nerve which had been frayed raw by a century of abuse and betrayal: the treaty-trust relationship between Indians and the Federal Government.

Hickel's remarks at Seattle and on the water problems in Nevada prior to the meeting of the National Congress of American Indians fitted exactly into prior speeches and problems of other times and places which had resulted in policies and programs destructive of the reservation communities. He could not have said anything more inflammatory than that the Federal Government had been "over-protective" of Indian rights, implying that the Government would be less zealous in fulfilling his responsibilities during his tenure as Secretary of the Interior.

Had Hickel been thoroughly briefed on the sterling record his predecessors had achieved, it is doubtful that he would have made the "over-protective" statement. The Government has been over-protective of Indian rights only in the sense that John Dillinger "over-protected" banks by robbing them before other criminals showed up.

In 1908 the Supreme Court decided the case of *Winters* v. *United States* in which Indian water rights were given priority over any other rights on streams running through Indian reservations. It has been clear, therefore, for most of this century, that the Pyramid Lake Paiutes have first priority for sufficient water in the Truckee-Carson river system to stabilize their lake *at the level at which it stood when the reservation was established.* Yet Interior had watched as the Indian water went elsewhere and the lake declined precipitously each year.

In 1924 the Secretary of the Interior was authorized to construct the Coolidge Dam in Arizona. In the authorizing legislation it clearly stated that the project was "for the purpose, first, of providing water for the irrigation of lands allotted to Pima Indians on the Gila River Reservation, Arizona." The Federal Government delivered just about enough water for Ira Hayes, Pima Indian and Marine hero of Iwo Jima, to drown in. Never was there any good faith by the Government to help the Indians irrigate their lands. Consequently, the water made available by the project went to non-Indians residing off the reservation.

With water the crucial element in the development of Indian reservations, the concept of "over-protection" appears nonsensical in view of the fact that, attached to every major Interior Department appropriation bill is a little rider stating that no Federal funds can go to develop the water rights of the tribes in California, Oregon and Nevada. Indian reservations thus lie dormant and undeveloped in those states, while non-Indians have sufficient water to develop their own lands.

To add to the irony of the "over-protection" which Indian people supposedly receive is the fact that, when the United States has to deal with foreign nations, it presents a clean and pious front. In 1913 the case of the Cayuga Nation, member of the Iroquois League, came before the American-British Claims Arbitration. The British Government wanted just compensation from the United States under the provisions of the Peace of Utrecht for lands which the state of New York took from the Cayugas after the War of 1812.

In the appendix to the answer filed by the United States to the British complaint, the Government declared:

> *Under that system the Indians residing within the United States are so far independent that they live under their own customs and not under the laws of the United States; that their rights upon the lands which they inhabit or hunt are secured to them by boundaries defined in amicable treaties between the United States and themselves; and that whenever those boundaries are varied, it is also by amicable and voluntary treaties, by which they receive from the United States ample compensation for every right they have to the lands ceded by them.*

Traditionally, Indian tribes had been treated in this manner. They were early regarded as distinct and sovereign nations fully capable of entering into compacts, agreements and contracts with the United

States. The Delaware Treaty of 1778, the earliest published treaty, spoke of "peace and friendship" which was necessary between the peoples of the United States and the tribe. It described the Delawares as being "dependent upon the (United States) for all articles of clothing, utensils and implements of war." It was fundamentally a trade agreement.

Until 1871 the tribes were treated as sovereign yet dependent domestic nations with whom the Federal Government was bound to treat for land cessions. In the treaties, the Government accepted the responsibility to protect the lands reserved by the tribes for their own use against encroachments by its own citizens. In that year, however, Congress decided that it would sign no more treaties with tribes. Instead, a policy emerged aimed at breaking up the tribal structures, even though the United States had promised in good faith that it would not interfere with traditional tribal customs and laws.

The shift in policy placed major emphasis on enticing, threatening, or deceiving individual Indians into forsaking their tribal relations. A comparable situation would exist if the Government refused to recognize General Motors as a corporation and insisted that it would become concerned with the individual stockholders, enticing them to sell their stock and liquidating the assets of the corporation, all the while wondering why General Motors was declining as an economic entity.

The tribes fought back. Asserting that the treaties were contracts between two parties, the tribe and the Federal Government, they often punished with death any leaders who signed away tribal rights. While fundamental logic supported the tribal position, overwhelming power and deceit by Government officials were able to carry the day. The treaties had been signed by nations, not an arbitrary conglomerate of individuals. Yet the official Federal policy was to assimilate individual Indians even if their rights as members of tribes had to be breached.

A major influence against the tribes was the ideology of the missionaries who were attempting to force their own ideas of culture on the captive audiences on the reservations. The missionaries believed that only by inculcating selfishness and the concept of private property into tribal society would individual Indians be able to become Christians and be saved.

Church pressure to individualize the tribes and dispose of the tribal land estate resulted in the passage of the Dawes Act in 1887. This act divided the reservations up into allotments of 160 acres, and each Indian was given a piece of land for farming. The remainder of the tribal holdings was declared "surplus" and opened to settlement by non-Indians.

Before allotment was forced on the tribes, there was no poverty on the reservations. The minority report issued against the policy mentioned the complete absence of pauperism among the Five Civilized Tribes of Oklahoma. It suggested that the Indian method of holding land for an entire community might be superior to the idea of non-Indian society, in that this method precluded a class of people that was perennially poor, while non-Indian society was plagued with poverty in its lower economic class.

The effect of individualizing the tribal estate was the creation of extreme poverty on many of the reservations. Individualizing Indians unaccustomed to viewing land as a commodity were easily swindled out of their allotments. Good farm land often went for a bottle of liquor, white trustees of individual Indian estates often mysteriously inherited their wards' property, and dying Indians were known to have mysteriously given their lands to churches before expiring. One Indian commissioner trod on eggshells during his term because a half-million-dollar Indian estate passed on to a missionary society instead of to the Indian heirs. Between 1887 and 1934 some 90 million acres of land left Indian ownership in a variety of ways. The actual circumstances in some cases have never seen the light of day.

Indians who sold their lands did not merge into white society and disappear. They simply moved onto their relatives' lands and remained within the tribal society. Thus, the land base was rapidly diminishing while the population continued to remain constant and, in some cases, grew spectacularly.

The situation had become so bad by 1926 that a massive study was authorized. It was called the Meriam Survey, and it pointed out that if the allotment process was not solved, the United States would soon have on its hands a landless, pauperized Indian population totally incapable of succeeding in American society.

In 1933, the New Deal Administration appointed John Collier as Indian Affairs Commissioner. He helped to write into law the basic charter of Indian rights called the Indian Reorganization Act. Indian tribes were given status as Federal corporations under this act, allotment was stopped and efforts were made to rebuild a land base for the Indian communities.

Tribal governments allocated a substantial portion of tribal income to purchase the allotments of individual Indians, thus holding in Indian hands the land that would have been lost forever. Tribes began their gradual revival of traditional ways, and were making excellent progress when World War II caused a dreadful reduction in domestic spending. Programs could not be funded until after the war.

In 1954 the chairmanship of the Indian Subcommittee of the Senate Interior Committee was taken over by Senator Arthur Watkins of Utah. Watkins was an archconservative who understood nothing of Indian treaties, was contemptuous of Indian people, and was determined to solve the "Indian problem" in his short tenure as chairman of the committee. He began a unilateral war against Indian communities that was known as "termination."

Watkins visualized himself as the Abraham Lincoln of the 20th century. Characterizing the reservations as havens of irresponsibility, and accepting the thesis that the Federal Government had been too protective of Indian rights, the Senator was determined to break the long-standing commitments of the United States to its Indian tribes—whether it was just or not.

"With the aim of 'equality before the law' in mind, our course should rightly be no other," Watkins announced. "Firm and constant consideration for those of Indian ancestry should lead us all to work diligently with all other Americans. Following in the footsteps of the Emancipation Proclamation of 94 years ago, I see the following words emblazoned in letters of fire above the heads of the Indians—THESE PEOPLE SHALL BE FREE."

If Watkins was determined to *free* the Indians, he was a generation too late. In 1924 the Indian Citizens Act was passed making all non-citizen Indians American citizens with full rights and privileges. The act further declared that the "granting of such citizenship shall not in any manner impair or otherwise affect the right of any Indians to tribal or other property."

The Indian Citizens Act thus gave full constitutional rights to individual Indians insofar as they were individuals. It specifically exempted any rights that individual Indians may have had in tribal property from its operation. The dual citizenship of Indian people was thus recognized.

But Watkins was convinced that holding an interest in tribal property in addition to holding citizenship was a handicap. Under this theory, everyone who benefited from a trust fund was automatically a second-class citizen.

A number of tribes fell victim to Watkins's crusade. The Menominees owned a forest in Wisconsin. They had a tribal sawmill and operated it to provide employment for tribal members, rather than to make a profit—although with their exemption from corporate taxation they often showed a profit. The tribe spent most of its income on social services, supporting its own hospital and providing its own law enforcement on the reservation. It was more genuinely a self-supporting community than many non-Indian communities near it.

Termination of Federal supervision meant an immediate tax bill of 55 per cent on the sawmill. To meet this, the sawmill had to be automated, thus throwing a substantial number of Indians out of work and onto the unemployment rolls. To meet the rising unemployment situation, the only industry, the sawmill, had to be taxed by the county. There was an immediate spiral downward in the capital structure of the tribe so that, in the years since the termination bill was passed, it has had to receive some $10-million in special state and Federal aid. The end is not yet in sight.

When the smoke had cleared, some 8,000 Indians had been deprived of rights their grandfathers had dearly purchased through land cessions. The Paiutes of Utah and Klamaths of Oregon were caught in a private trusteeship more restrictive than their original Federal trust relationship, from which they were to have been "freed." Fortunately, Texas made a tourist attraction out of the Alabama-Coushatta reservation in that state, thus preserving most of the tribal assets. The mixed-blood Utes of Utah formed their own organization and tried to remain together as a community. The Siletz and Grande Ronde Indians of Oregon, the California Indians, and the Catawbas of South Carolina simply vanished. Menominee County became the most depressed county in the nation.

In Watkins's mind, and in the mind of his successors on the Senate Interior Committee, the opportunity to remake American Indians into small businessmen was too much of a temptation. The termination policy continued to roll in spite of its catastrophic effects on the Indian communities.

Tribes refused to consider any programs, feeling that it was no use to build good houses when the reservation might be sold out from under them at any time. Development schemes to upgrade reservation resources were turned down by people with no apparent future. The progress which had been made by the tribes under the Indian Reorganization Act ground to a halt. Indian people spent a decade in limbo, hesitant to make any plans for fear they would come under attack by the irrational policy.

Watkins's rationale at the beginning had been that he was making the individual Indians first-class citizens, where they previously had been handicapped by maintaining their tribal relationships. It was the same reasoning that had led policy-makers in the last century to force allotment on the tribes and create the original poverty conditions on the reservations. When the termination legislation was finally drawn for the Menominees, the concluding phrase in section 10 of the bill was illuminating: "Nothing in this act shall affect the status of the members of the tribe as citizens of the United States"!

The argument of "freeing" the Indians was as phony as could be.

The act did nothing but dissipate tribal capital and destroy the rights of Indian tribes to have their own communities. But termination fitted exactly into the integrationist-thought world of the period, and the expanding civil rights movement of the black community, which had been given impetus by the decision of *Brown* v. *Topeka Board of Education*, the famous school desegregation case of 1954. So it *seemed* the right thing to do.

Society has come a long way in its understanding of itself since 1954. The ensuing civil rights movement, which had shaken the foundations of society during the nineteen-fifties, changed abruptly into the black power movements of the late sixties. For half a decade we have been struggling to define the place of a group of people in American society and, as numerous reports have indicated, the divisions in the society have become more pronounced, the hatreds more violent and lasting.

Termination slowed down during the Kennedy-Johnson Administrations, but the basic congressional directive has never been changed. Policy-makers in Congress and in the Interior Department continue to regard decisions made in haste in 1954 as imperatives which they must follow today. Only by a vigilant National Congress of American Indians watching the Washington scene day and night have Indian people been able to stop further implementation of this policy.

Walter Hickel, in his casual remarks, stirred up a hornet's nest of Indian concern. It did not seem possible to tribal leaders that the new administration would return to a policy proven bankrupt when it was applied to their land holdings in 1887, again proven bankrupt in 1954 with the further dissipation of their remaining lands and resources, and completely out of tune with the social movements of today.

Indian tribes have been able, in spite of all pressures exerted against them, and the failure of the Federal Government to defend their rights, to maintain a capital in land and resources by which they can maintain their own communities. They have been able to keep tribal governments alive and functioning. In the War on Poverty, tribes provided services for all people within reservation boundaries, red or white, and many children received services that they would not have otherwise received because their counties did not want to sponsor programs under the Office of Economic Opportunity.

The record of Indian people as a recognized self-governing community is enlightening. The progress of the last decade is spectacular and sophisticated for a people with a national average of eight years of education. Indian people are now demanding control of education programs through the creation of Indian reservation school boards. They are certain they can do better than either the state or Federal education they have been given in the past. The variety of projects undertaken by Indian communities is staggering and encompasses everything from sawmills to ocean-going fishing vessels, motels to carpet factories.

American society has much to learn from Indian tribes. It may all be lost if another era of struggle over reservation existence is initiated. The black community, spearheaded by the demands for reparations by James Forman, is desperately seeking capital funds. Indian tribes already have capital in land and resources and have demonstrated how well it can be used.

Blacks and Mexicans are developing rural cooperatives in an effort to solve the poverty of their people in the rural areas. Indian tribes have already proven that rural corporations and cooperatives can and do work when undertaken by a united community.

Conservationists are pointing out the rapidly dwindling natural resources of the nation, the danger of total extinction of life unless strong conservation practices are begun at once. The Quinault and Lummi Indian tribes have already zoned their beaches to conserve their natural state, while the White Mountain Apaches have developed nearly 30 artificial lakes and maintain the best fishing and recreation areas in Arizona.

The power movements, the Amish situation in the Midwest, the desire of the Acadians in Louisiana to have French taught in schools, the conflict between the ethnic groups in the urban areas, all point toward new social concepts revolving around a number of ethnic and racial communities desiring to conduct their own affairs. Even the rising conservative trend in politics seeks power at the local level rather than continued direction from long distance.

Tribes have overcome enmities of the past. They were once far deeper and more bitter than in the current impasse between black and white. Unemployment is declining as tribal programs are committed to creating jobs, not simply making profits. Land is being renewed, beaches and rivers are being cleared and the reservations are becoming models of proper land use. Indian society is stabilizing itself to face the instantaneous electric world of today far better than are other segments of American society.

The Indian outrage at Hickel was a cry to society at large. "If you destroy us," it really said, "you will destroy your last chance to understand who you are, where you have been, and where you have to go next in order to survive as a people." One hopes Secretary Hickel and the Senators and Congressmen will hear the cry and understand.

This Country Was a Lot Better Off when the Indians Were Running It. Vine Deloria, Jr. | On Nov. 9,
1969, a contingent of American Indians, led by Adam Nordwall, a Chippewa from Minnesota, and Richard Oakes, a Mohawk from New York, landed on Alcatraz Island in San Francisco Bay and claimed the 13-acre rock "by right of discovery." The island had been abandoned six and a half years ago, and although there had been various suggestions concerning its disposal nothing had been done to make use of the land. Since there are Federal treaties giving some tribes the right to abandoned Federal property within a tribe's original territory, the Indians of the Bay area felt that they could lay claim to the island.

For nearly a year the United Bay Area Council of American Indians, a confederation of urban Indian organizations, had been talking about submitting a bid for the island to use it as a West Coast Indian cultural

SOURCE: New York Times Sunday Magazine, March 8, 1970.

center and vocational training headquarters. Then, on Nov. 1, the San Francisco American Indian Center burned down. The center had served an estimated 30,000 Indians in the immediate area and was the focus of activities of the urban Indian community. It became a matter of urgency after that and, as Adam Nordwall said, "it was GO." Another landing, on Nov. 20, by nearly 100 Indians in a swift midnight raid secured the island.

The new inhabitants have made "the Rock" a focal point symbolic of Indian people. Under extreme difficulty they have worked to begin repairing sanitary facilities and buildings. The population has been largely transient, many people have stopped by, looked the situation over for a few days, then gone home, unwilling to put in the tedious work necessary to make the island support a viable community.

The Alcatraz news stories are somewhat shocking to non-Indians. It is difficult for most Americans to comprehend that there still exists a living community of nearly one million Indians in this country. For many people, Indians have become a species of movie actor periodically dispatched to the Happy Hunting Grounds by John Wayne on the "Late. Late Show." Yet there are some 315 Indian tribal groups in 26 states still functioning as quasi-sovereign nations under treaty status; they range from the mammoth Navajo tribe of some 132,000 with 16 million acres of land to tiny Mission Creek of California with 15 people and a tiny parcel of property. There are over half a million Indians in the cities alone, with the largest concentrations in San Francisco, Los Angeles, Minneapolis and Chicago.

The take-over of Alcatraz is to many Indian people a demonstration of pride in being Indian and a dignified, yet humorous, protest against current conditions existing on the reservations and in the cities. It is this special pride and dignity, the determination to judge life according to one's own values, and the unconquerable conviction that the tribes will not die that has always characterized Indian people as I have known them.

I was born in Martin, a border town on the Pine Ridge Indian Reservation in South Dakota, in the midst of the Depression. My father was an Indian missionary who served 18 chapels on the eastern half of the reservation. In 1934, when I was 1, the Indian Reorganization Act was passed, allowing Indian tribes full rights of self-government for the first time since the late eighteen-sixties. Ever since those days, when the Sioux had agreed to forsake the life of the hunter for that of the farmer, they had been systematically deprived of any voice in decisions affecting their lives and property. Tribal ceremonies and religious practices were forbidden. The reservation was fully controlled by men in Washington, most of whom had never visited a reservation and felt no urge to do so.

The first years on the reservations were extremely hard for the Sioux. Kept confined behind fences they were almost wholly dependent upon Government rations for their food supply. Many died of hunger and malnutrition. Game was scarce and few were allowed to have weapons for fear of another Indian war. In some years there was practically no food available. Other years, rations were withheld until the men agreed to farm the tiny pieces of land each family had been given. In desperation many families were forced to eat stray dogs and cats to keep alive.

By World War I, however, many of the Sioux families had developed prosperous ranches. Then the Government stepped in, sold the Indians' cattle for wartime needs, and after the war leased the grazing land to whites, creating wealthy white ranchers and destitute Indian landlords.

With the passage of the Indian Reorganization Act, native ceremonies and practices were given full recognition by Federal authorities. My earliest memories are of trips along dusty roads to Kyle, a small settlement in the heart of the reservation, to attend the dances. Ancient men, veterans of battles even then considered footnotes to the settlement of the West, brought their costumes out of hiding and walked about the grounds gathering the honors they had earned half a century before. They danced as if the intervening 50 years had been a lost weekend from which they had fully recovered. I remember best Dewey Beard, then in his late 80's and a survivor of the Little Big Horn. Even at that late date Dewey was hesitant to speak of the battle for fear of reprisal. There was no doubt, as one watched the people's expressions, that the Sioux had survived their greatest ordeal and were ready to face whatever the future might bring.

In those days the reservation was isolated and unsettled. Dirt roads held the few mail routes together. One could easily get lost in the wild back country as roads turned into cowpaths without so much as a backward glance. Remote settlements such as Buzzard Basin and Cuny Table were nearly inaccessible. In the spring every bridge on the reservation would be washed out with the first rain and would remain out until late summer. But few people cared. Most of the reservation people, traveling by team and wagon, merely forded the creeks and continued their journey, almost contemptuous of the need for roads and bridges.

The most memorable event of my early childhood was visiting Wounded Knee where 200 Sioux, including women and children, were slaughtered in 1890 by troopers of the Seventh Cavalry in what is believed to have been a delayed act of vengeance for Custer's defeat. The people were simply lined up and shot down much as was allegedly done, according to newspaper reports, at Songmy. The wounded were left to die in a three-day Dakota blizzard, and when the soldiers returned to the scene after the storm some were still alive and were saved. The massacre was vividly etched in the minds of many of the older reservation people, but it was difficult to find anyone who wanted to talk about it.

Many times, over the years, my father would point out survivors of the massacre, and people on the reservation always went out of their way to help them. For a long time there was a bill in Congress to pay indemnities to the survivors, but the War Department always insisted that it had been a "battle" to stamp out the Ghost Dance religion among the Sioux. This does not, however, explain bayoneted Indian women and children found miles from the scene of the incident.

Strangely enough, the Depression was good for Indian reservations, particularly for the people at Pine Ridge. Since their lands had been leased to non-Indians by the Bureau of Indian Affairs, they had only a small rent check and the contempt of those who leased their lands to show for their ownership. But the Federal programs devised to solve the national economic crisis were also made available to Indian people, and there was work available for the first time in the history of the reservations.

The Civilian Conservation Corps set up a camp on the reservation and many Indians were hired under the program. In the canyons north of Allen, S.D., a beautiful buffalo pasture was built by the C.C.C, and the whole area was transformed into a recreation wonderland. Indians would come from miles around to see the buffalo and leave with a strange look in their eyes. Many times I stood silently watching while old men talked to the buffalo about the old days. They would conclude by singing a song before respectfully departing, their eyes filled with tears and their minds occupied with the memories of other times and places. It was difficult to determine who was the captive—the buffalo fenced in or the Indian fenced out.

While the rest of America suffered from the temporary deprivation of its luxuries, Indian people had a period of prosperity, as it were. Paychecks were regular. Small cattle herds were started, cars were purchased, new clothes and necessities became available. To a people who had struggled along on $50 cash income per year, the C.C.C. was the greatest program ever to come along. The Sioux had climbed from absolute deprivation to mere poverty, and this was the best time the reservation ever had.

World War II ended this temporary prosperity. The C.C.C camps were closed; reservation programs were cut to the bone and social services became virtually non-existent; "Victory gardens" were suddenly the style, and people began to be aware that a great war was being waged overseas.

The war dispersed the reservation people as nothing ever had. Every day, it seemed, we would be bidding farewell to families as they headed west to work in the defense plants on the coast.

A great number of Sioux people went west and many of the Sioux on Alcatraz today are their children and relatives. There may now be as many Sioux in California as there are on the reservations in South Dakota because of the great wartime migration.

Those who stayed on the reservation had the war brought directly to their doorstep when they were notified that their sons had to go across the seas and fight. Busloads of Sioux boys left the reservation for parts unknown. In many cases even the trip to nearby Martin was a new experience for them, let alone training in Texas, California or Colorado. There were always going-away ceremonies conducted by the older people who admonished the boys to uphold the old tribal traditions and not to fear death. It was not death they feared but living with an unknown people in a distant place.

I was always disappointed with the Government's way of handling Indian servicemen. Indians were simply lost in the shuffle of a million men in uniform. Many boys came home on furlough and feared to return. They were not cowards in any sense of the word but the loneliness and boredom of stateside duty were crushing their spirits. They spent months without seeing another Indian. If the Government had recruited all-Indian outfits it would have easily solved this problem and also had the best fighting units in the world at its disposal. I often wonder what an all-Sioux or Apache company, painted and singing its songs, would have done to the morale of élite German panzer units.

After the war Indian veterans straggled back to the reservations and tried to pick up their lives. It was very difficult for them to resume a life of poverty after having seen the affluent outside world. Some spent a few days with the old folks and then left again for the big cities. Over the years they have emerged as leaders of the urban Indian movement. Many of their children are the nationalists of today who are adamant about keeping the reservations they have visited only on vacations. Other veterans stayed on the reservations and entered tribal politics.

The reservations radically changed after the war. During the Depression there were about five telephones in Martin. If there was a call for you, the man at the hardware store had to come down to your house and get you to answer it. A couple of years after the war a complete dial system was installed that extended to most of the smaller communities on the reservation. Families that had been hundreds of miles from any form of communication were now only minutes away from a telephone.

Roads were built connecting the major communities of the Pine Ridge country. No longer did it take hours to go from one place to another. With these kinds of roads everyone had to have a car. The team and wagon vanished, except for those families who lived at various "camps" in inaccessible canyons pretty much as their ancestors had. (Today, even they have adopted the automobile for traveling long distances in search of work.)

I left the reservation in 1951 when my family moved to Iowa. I went back only once for an extended stay, in the summer of 1955, while on a furlough, and after that I visited only occasionally during summer vacations. In the meantime, I attended college, served a hitch in the Marines, and went to the seminary. After I graduated from the seminary, I took a job with the United Scholarship Service, a private organization devoted to the college and secondary-school education of American Indian and Mexican students. I had spent my last two years of high school in an Eastern preparatory school and so was probably the only Indian my age who knew what an independent Eastern school was like. As the program developed, we soon had some 30 students placed in Eastern schools.

I insisted that all the students who entered the program be able to qualify for scholarships as students and not simply as Indians. I was pretty sure we could beat the white man at his own educational game, which seemed to me the only way to gain his respect. I was soon to find that this was a dangerous attitude to have. The very people who were supporting the program—non-Indians in the national church establishment—accused me of trying to form a colonialist "élite" by insisting that only kids with strong test scores and academic patterns be sent east to school. They wanted to continue the ancient pattern of soft-hearted paternalism toward Indians. I didn't feel we should cry our way into the schools; that sympathy would destroy the students we were trying to help.

In 1964, while attending the annual convention of the National Congress of American Indians, I was elected its executive director. I learned more about life in the N.C.A.I. in three years than I had in the previous 30. Every conceivable problem that could occur in an Indian society was suddenly thrust at me from 315 different directions. I discovered that I was one of the people who were supposed to solve the problems. The only trouble was that Indian people locally and on the national level were being played off one against the other by clever whites who had either ego or income at stake. While there were many feasible solutions, few could be tried without whites with vested interests working night and day to destroy the unity we were seeking on a national basis.

In the mid-nineteen-sixties, the whole generation that had grown up after World War II and had left the reservations during the fifties to get an education was returning to Indian life as "educated Indians." But we soon knew better. Tribal societies had existed for centuries without going outside themselves for education and information. Yet many of us thought that we would be able to improve the traditional tribal methods. We were wrong.

For three years we ran around the conference circuit attending numerous meetings called to "solve" the Indian problems. We listened to and spoke with anthropologists, historians, sociologists, psychologists, economists, educators and missionaries. We worked with many Government agencies and with every conceivable doctrine, idea and program ever created. At the end of this happy round of consultations the reservation people were still plodding along on their own time schedule, doing the things they considered important. They continued to solve their problems their way in spite of the advice given them by "Indian experts."

By 1967 there was a radical change in thinking on the part of many of us. Conferences were proving unproductive. Where non-Indians had been pushed out to make room for Indian people, they had wormed their way back into power and again controlled the major programs serving Indians. The poverty programs, reservation and university technical assistance groups were dominated by whites who had pushed Indian administrators aside.

Reservation people, meanwhile, were making steady progress in spite of the numerous setbacks suffered by the national Indian community. So, in large part, younger Indian leaders who had been playing the national conference field began working at the local level to build community movements from the ground up. By consolidating local organizations into power groups they felt that they would be in a better position to influence national thinking.

Robert Hunter, director of the Nevada Intertribal Council, had already begun to build a strong state organization of tribes and communities. In South Dakota, Gerald One Feather, Frank LaPointe and Ray Briggs formed the American Indian Leadership Conference, which quickly welded the educated young Sioux in that state into a strong regional organization active in nearly every phase of Sioux life. Gerald is now running for the prestigious post of chairman of the Oglala Sioux, the largest Sioux tribe, numbering some 15,000 members. Ernie Stevens, an Oneida from Wisconsin, and Lee Cook, a Chippewa from Minnesota, developed a strong program for economic and community development in Arizona. Just recently Ernie has moved into the post of director of the California Intertribal Council, a statewide organization representing some 130,000 California Indians in cities and on the scattered reservations of that state.

By the fall of 1967, it was apparent that the national Indian scene was collapsing in favor of strong regional organizations, although the National Congress of American Indians and the National Indian Youth Council continued to grow. There was yet another factor emerging on the Indian scene; the old-timers of the Depression days had educated a group of younger Indians in the old ways and these people were now becoming a major force in Indian life. Led by Thomas Banyaca of the Hopi, Mad Bear Anderson of the Tuscaroras, Clifton Hill of the Creeks, and Rolling Thunder of the Shoshones, the traditional Indians were forcing the whole Indian community to rethink its understanding of Indian life.

The message of the traditionalists is simple. They demand a return to basic Indian philosophy, establishment of ancient methods of government by open council instead of elected officials, a revival of Indian religions and replacement of white laws with Indian customs; in short, a complete return to the ways of the old people. In an age dominated by tribalizing communications media, their message makes a great deal of sense.

But in some areas their thinking is opposed to that of the National Congress of American Indians, which represents officially elected tribal governments organized under the Indian Reorganization Act as Federal corporations. The contemporary problem is therefore one of defining the meaning of "tribe." Is it a traditionally organized band of Indians following customs with medicine men and chiefs dominating the policies of the tribe, or is it a modern corporate structure attempting to compromise at least in part with modern white culture?

The problem has been complicated by private foundations' and Government agencies' funding of Indian programs. In general this process, although it has brought a great amount of money into Indian country, has been one of cooptation. Government agencies must justify their appropriation requests every year and can only take chances on spectacular programs that will serve as showcases of progress. They are not willing to invest the capital funds necessary to build viable self-supporting communities on the reservations because these programs do not have an immediate publicity potential. Thus, the Government agencies are forever committed to conducting conferences to discover that one "key" to Indian life that will give them the edge over their rival agencies in the annual appropriations derby.

Churches and foundations have merely purchased an Indian leader or program that conforms with their ideas of what Indian people should be doing. The large foundations have bought up the well-dressed, handsome "new image" Indian who is comfortable in the big cities but virtually helpless at an Indian meeting. Churches have given money to Indians who have been willing to copy black militant activist tactics, and the more violent and insulting the Indian can be, the more the churches seem to love it. They are wallowing in self-guilt and piety over the lot of the poor, yet funding demagogues of their own choosing to speak for the poor.

I did not run for re-election as executive director of the N.C.A.I. in the fall of 1967, but entered law school at the University of Colorado instead. It was apparent to me that the Indian revolution was well under way and that someone had better get a legal education so that we could have our own legal program for defense of Indian treaty rights. Thanks to a Ford Foundation program, nearly 50 Indians are now in law school, assuring the Indian community of legal talent in the years ahead. Within four years I foresee another radical shift in Indian leadership patterns as the growing local movements are affected by the new Indian lawyers.

There is an increasing scent of victory in the air in Indian country these days. The mood is comparable to the old days of the Depression when the men began to dance once again. As the Indian movement gathers momentum and individual Indians cast their lot with the tribe, it will become apparent that not only will Indians survive the electronic world of Marshall McLuhan, they will thrive in it. At the present time everyone is watching how mainstream America will handle the issues of pollution, poverty, crime and racism when it does not fundamentally understand the issues. Knowing the importance of tribal survival, Indian people are speaking more and more of sovereignty, of the great political technique of the open council, and of the need for gaining the community's consensus on all programs before putting them into effect.

One can watch this same issue emerge in white society as the "Woodstock Nation," the "Blackstone Nation" and the block organizations are developed. This is a full tribalizing process involving a nontribal people, and it is apparent that some people are frightened by it. But it is the kind of social phenomenon upon which Indians feast.

In 1965 I had a long conversation with an old Papago. I was trying to get the tribe to pay its dues to the National Congress of American Indians and I had asked him to speak to the tribal council for me. He said that he would but that the Papagos didn't really need the N.C.A.I. They were like, he told me, the old mountain in the distance. The Spanish had come and dominated them for 300 years and then left. The Mexicans had come and ruled them for a century, but they also left. "The Americans," he said, "have been here only about 80 years. They, too, will vanish, but the Papagos and the mountain will always be here."

This attitude and understanding of life is what American society is searching for.

I wish the Government would give Alcatraz to the Indians now occupying it. They want to create five centers on the island. One center would be for a North American studies program; another would be a spiritual and medical center where Indian religions and medicines would be used and studied. A third center would concentrate on ecological studies based on an Indian view of nature—that man should live with the land and not simply on it. A job-training center and a museum would also be founded on the island. Certain of these programs would obviously require Federal assistance.

Some people may object to this approach, yet, Health, Education and Welfare gave out $10-million last year to non-Indians to study Indians. Not one single dollar went to an Indian scholar or researcher to present the point of view of Indian people. And the studies done by non-Indians added nothing to what was already known about Indians.

Indian people have managed to maintain a viable and cohesive social order in spite of everything the non-Indian society has thrown at them in an effort to break the tribal structure. At the same time, non-Indian society has created a monstrosity of a culture where people starve while the granaries are filled and the sun can never break through the smog.

By making Alcatraz an experimental Indian center operated and planned by Indian people, we would be given a chance to see what we could do toward developing answers to modern social problems. Ancient tribalism can be incorporated with modern technology in an urban setting. Perhaps we would not succeed in the effort, but the Government is spending billions every year and still the situation is rapidly growing worse. It just seems to a lot of Indians that this continent was a lot better off when we were running it.

A Note from the Editors

Beginning in the 1960's a new challenge began to be addressed to the legitimacy of the tribal governments that had been organized under the Indian Reorganization Act and other legislation. Nationalistic and radical organizations, such as the National Indian Youth Council (NIYC) and the American Indian Movement (AIM), criticized these governments on several grounds. First, they noted critically that some tribal executives were being appointed by the president of the United States, rather than being chosen by the Indian peoples themselves. By the 1970's their criticism had resulted in some modification of the practice of appointment and the introduction of some electoral processes. But, and here was a second criticism of these organizations, among a number of Indian tribes, the tribal electorate included many persons who were only marginally of Indian blood while excluding many persons of indubitable Indian ancestry and conduct. The most extreme case was the Osage, but it was also true that the electoral process recently introduced among the Oklahoma Cherokee was including many persons who were only marginally of Indian ancestry and culture. Third, these radical organizations contended that the very process of representative government and of elections was foreign to Indian traditions of tribal decision-making, which were predicated on discussion that continued until unanimity was reached. The white (Western) system of representative government and coercive authority was foreign to Indians, so that the offices tended to be captured and utilized by persons who were "white" or assimilated in their orientation. Fourth, it was argued that many tribal governments had been brought under the domination of the U.S. Bureau of Indian Affairs, so that they represented the wishes of federal bureaucrats and not of Indian peoples.

Since the Indian New Deal of John Collier and his associates, the Bureau of Indian Affairs had structured its relationships to many Indian peoples via their tribal governments. Moreover, the major national Indian interest organization, the National Council of American Indians, was essentially constituted as the union of tribal governments. Thus, the most powerful spokesmen for Indians, and the most powerful federal agency dealing with Indians, were both predicated on the permanence of tribal governments and their representation of Indian interests. Yet, as more and more Indians came to migrate to urban areas, their interests were decreasingly represented by tribal governments. Hence the appeal of radical and nationalistic organizations, such as NIYC and AIM, in their denunciation of both tribal governments and the BIA. If Indians were to be represented to the U.S. government as Indians, even while living in urban centers, then new relationships would have to be established. When AIM occupied BIA offices in Washington, D.C., during 1971 and then "seized" Wounded Knee on the Pine Ridge Reservation in 1972, its demands and actions struck responsive chords among urbanized Indians.

VII

RELIGIOUS
PAN-INDIANISM:
Indian Life
Is Not a Business

The Native American Church (NAC) means just that: a church for native Americans, Indians. Participants in this church will say that Christianity is for whites, but peyote is for Indians. This does not mean that they reject Christianity, for some individuals may be parishioners of a Protestant denomination and participants in the NAC. It is common for an NAC service to incorporate Christian symbolism and moralism. Indeed, at the turn of the century, before the organized Christian denominations had committed themselves against peyote, some of these cults regarded themselves as Christian denominations; among the Oto Indians of Oklahoma, the peyotists incorporated themselves as "The First-born Church of Christ." One reason that such names were abandoned was that they did not indicate clearly enough that Indians were organizing themselves for their own religious purposes; and while Indians were eager to accept pertinent Christian teachings and symbols, they were not willing to submit themselves to the dogmatic leadership of the white (or Indian) enemies of peyote.

Because both Indians and whites concentrate on the role of peyote and the independence of the NAC from the Christian denominational structure, they are apt to overlook a profound similarity in organizational form—the open congregational format. Before the invasions of the whites, the religious activities of Indians were organized on a tribal basis and revolved about the spiritual and physical well-being of the tribe, or band, and its members. There was neither circumstance nor reason for Indians of different tribes to come together in worship. Then, in North America these tribal religious systems went into decline with the confinement on the reservations, the destruction of the traditional ecological adaptations, and the campaigns by government agents and missionaries against traditional ceremonials. Many reservation Indians could not find adequate meaning and value in the Christianity preached by the missionaries, and the peyote cult spread from the Southwest across the plains.

While members of the NAC will use peyote privately for therapeutic purposes, the most typical and desired form of consumption is during the night ceremonial meeting. The NAC is congregational, and the congregants may be Indians of any tribe. In urban locales, the congregation will frequently contain members from different tribal and geographic backgrounds. Even in the ritual attended by Peter Nabokov in an isolated location on the Navajo reservation in Arizona, there were two Pawnee visiting from Oklahoma. A predominant rationale for such travel is to transport peyote. Indians from the Southwest will journey to the northern plains, bringing gifts of peyote to their coreligionists. Conversely, Indians from the North and East will journey to the Southwest in order to secure a supply for their rituals. Via such travel, there is much sociable and ritual interchange, so that, although the NAC lacks any dominant hierarchy or a central source of dogma, nonetheless there are strong similarities among all its congregations. As LaBarre notes, the essential ingredients of the peyote meal go back to pre-Columbian Mexico, but they can be found—suitably modified by circumstances and funds— among modern tribes in Montana.

The "Diabolic Root." Weston La-

Barre | Recently, the Supreme Court of California set aside the conviction of three Navaho Indians who had been arrested while engaged in a traditional religious ritual which involves the use of peyote—a cactus that contains, in small amounts, a moderately potent psychotropic substance called mescaline and that when eaten produces hallucinations in color. A court of appeals in California has previously upheld the original court's conviction, which imposed suspended sentence of two to ten years in jail on condition that the Indians give up this religious practice. The Supreme Court in reversing the judgments of the two lower courts, ruled that "to forbid the use of peyote is to remove the heart of peyotism" and so infringes the principle of religious freedom.

Peyote—the *raiz diabolica*, or "diabolic root"—is a small, carrot-shaped cactus, the gray-green top of which resembles a little dumpling or pincushion divided by curving radial ribs. The cactus has no spines, but atop the divisions made by the ribs are off-white tufts of matted fuzz, looking somewhat like small water-color brushes, from which peyote gets its neo-Greek botanical name, *Lophophora williamsii* ("crest bearer"). Cut off horizontally about ground level, this puffy top becomes the woody, bitter and weedy-tasting "peyote button." It grows wild in the Rio Grande valley and southwestward. (It should not, incidentally, be confused with mescal proper, from which beer and tequila are made, nor with the hallucinatory mushroom, called teonanacatl, nor with LSD.)

There are two stages in the physiological effects that result from eating peyote. First, the strychnine-like alkaloids in the cactus give a feeling of excitement and exhilaration like that induced by strong coffee. The face becomes flushed, the pupils dilate and the person tends to be talkative, light-headed and wakeful. (These alkaloids have been experimented with in pure form because of a possibility that they might be useful in treatment of heart disease.)

Later, the opposing alkaloids, chiefly mescaline, come into action and their effects last for 10 to 12 hours. Time perception is altered and a

SOURCE: *New York Times*, November 1, 1964.

curious sense of double existence occurs. One part of the mind remains critical and well-oriented, but when the eyes are closed and opened, elaborately beautiful designs are seen—fields of brilliantly colored jewels, vast and slowly changing geometrical constructions, occasionally the so-called "wall-paper effect," when diagonal lines of identical shapes change simultaneously as in a toy kaleidoscope.

Both Indians and whites have reported violently terrifying visions, like images of supernatural monsters. At other times, they have seen more comical monsters—a six-legged animal with ducks' heads for feet, for example, with each foot squawking ridiculously each time it is put down. Most impressive, probably, are scintillating aurora borealis scenes. Artists have said that their sense of color and design has been permanently heightened by peyote.

Other than visual hallucinations occasionally occur. One Indian member of the sect that uses peyote, the Native American Church, heard the sun come up with a gradually increasing roar. Another felt that the sound of a drum used in the ceremony lifted him up into the air. Some early writers have said that peyote is an aphrodisiac, and others just as firmly aver that it is anti-aphrodisiac, it is probably neither. There is no "hang-over" and no great toxic effects have been noted although sometimes, as with alcohol, Indians vomit from eating too many buttons at once.

Peyote is not habit-forming, for Indians often suddenly abandon peyotism and join a more Christianized church. After attending peyote rituals, and sometimes joining in them, on two field trips among Indian tribes, the writer has never used, nor felt the need to use, peyote during a quarter of a century. Some dozens of professional anthropologists who have studied peyotism would testify to the same effect. All authorities agree that peyote is not addictive.

Mexican tribes have used peyote since pre-Columbian times. Between 1870 and 1890 the peyote religion diffused via Southwestern Apaches and Texas Tonkawas, to the Comanche and Kiowa of the southern Great Plains. It has now spread over most Plains tribes as well as westward to the Washo of Nevada-California and northward to the Cree and other Canadian tribes. Peyotism is the main present-day native religion of more than 50 American Indian tribes including, among the best-known, the Cheyenne, Arapaho, Shawnee, Pawnee, Delaware, Osage, Ponca, Omaha, Winnebago, Kickapoo, Ute, Crow, Iowa, Paiute, Blackfoot and Chippewa. Among Siouans and Utah tribes, it has become much mixed with Christian elements, both Catholic and Protestant.

In the standard peyote meeting, the Indians enter a tepee about nightfall and pass clockwise to sit on a sagebrush-padded seat around a crescent-shaped earthen altar on which is an unusually large or fine peyote button. A fire is burning before the altar. The leader, or "Road Chief," sings the traditional Opening Song, holding a staff in his left hand and a medicine man's rattle in his right, to the drumming of the "Drum Chief" to his right. After the Road Chief directs the censing of communicants with smoke from cedar chips thrown onto the fire and everyone has made a prayer smoke (which must be of Bull Durham tobacco and should be made of oblong-cut cornhusks or dried blackjack oak leaves), peyote is passed around.

The meeting is continued as each man, in clockwise order sings four self-chosen peyote songs, holding the shaman's staff and rattle as his right-hand partner drums for him. Peyote songs are brisk rhythmic chants and are of three kinds: the Opening and three other ritual songs are in an unknown, archaic language, probably from the Southwest or Mexico; songs in the singer's tribal language, and Christianized songs (for example, "God, I thank You for all You have done for me through Jesus's name," and "God's Son says, 'Get up and follow Me.' ")

At midnight the Road Chief sings the Midnight Song, goes out of the tepee and blows an eagle wingbone whistle at the four corners of the compass. Singing then goes on again until dawn. The Road Chief then sings the Morning Song, whereupon his wife, representing "Peyote Woman," brings in a water bucket and bowls of parched corn in sugar water, fruit and boneless meat set in a west-to-east line before the altar. After prayer, each person partakes of the meal. This ritual, "peyote breakfast," dates back to prehistoric Mexico—and yet a modern Montana tribe was still ritually correct in serving corned beef, canned peaches and Cracker Jack!

Afterward, people lie around in the shade talking about their visual experiences and asking one another what they might mean. Perhaps someone has "caught" a new peyote song; another has had a vision which may predict good or bad luck ahead. Similar visions and events in the past are compared. At about noon a purely secular meal is served, and people go home, none the worse except for a sleepless night.

Some tribes, especially the Sioux, have an aboriginal custom of public confession of sin in the meeting; others cry with real tears in the old-fashioned way of prayer. The sick are doctored, the young admonished, a couple married, and the dead funeralized in peyote meetings. Any Indian is welcome and peyotism has become a pan-Indian movement, some tribes welcome Negroes, but only a trusted white man may attend.

What stand should a reasonable and well-informed person take toward the Indian cult? Missionaries, Indian agents, anthropologists, legislators and judges have differed in their answers.

Is peyotism "drug addiction in a religious disguise"? But it is a bona-fide traditional religion, and peyote is not addictive. Indians say they do not eat wafers and drink wine, but eat peyote and drink pure water. They say that "the white man goes into church and talks about Jesus, but the Indian goes into a tepee and talks to Jesus." Some cite the Bible, "And they shall eat the flesh in that night, roast with fire, and unleavened bread; and with bitter herbs they shall eat it" (Exodus xii, 8).

Since the liberal regime of John Collier, Franklin D. Roosevelt's Commissioner of Indian Affairs, government authorities have taken the lenient view of permitting Indians religious, as well as political, self-choice. Responsible legislators and judges have all, ultimately, taken a liberal permissive attitude also. Anthropologists, perhaps the persons best informed on the subject, have uniformly defended Indian rights.

As one anthropologist puts it, "There can be no shadow of a doubt concerning the deep and humble sincerity of the worship and belief—and sincerity perhaps, even in the absence of other ingredients, is the chief component of a living religion. And if the chief function of a religion is the liquidation of the anxieties and the solution of the fears and troubles of its adherents, then the peyote religion eminently qualifies as such . . . Western man already complacently accepts (since it is his) the mass use of substances such as tobacco and alcohol which, to physical health, can be far more dangerous than a weekly Indian use of a feebly psychotropic desert plant. And as for his mental health, Western man is already embedded in narcotic institutions such as advertising, television and movies—which invite illusions about ourselves fully as dangerous as any Indian religious cult."

Peyote and the Law

Virtually the only commercial sources of supply for peyote are a handful of Indian families in Texas, Arizona, and New Mexico who collect the cactus primarily for use by other Indians in religious ceremonies. Purchase of the drug by non-Indians in any large amounts is rare.

The use of peyote is forbidden in a number of states. There is no Federal law prohibiting such use, but the Food and Drug Administration has classified peyote as a drug (non-narcotic) that requires a doctor's prescription. Legally, the Federal Government's jurisdiction in this area is confined to instances wherein peyote is transported across state lines, directed to non-Indians who are obviously not obtaining it for use in religious ceremonies and just as obviously have not had it prescribed by a physician, since peyote has no medicinal value.

The Peyote Road. Peter Nabokov | WINDOW ROCK, Ariz.—The station wagon suddenly pulled off the dusty, unpaved road winding north from Fort Defiance, Arizona. The driver, a burly, middle-aged Navajo in rancher's hat, was wearing the adornments of a peyote devotee ready for an all-night meeting—cardinal red tie with silver stylized "water bird" clip, matching red socks. A

SOURCE: *New York Times*, March 9, 1969.

rectangular varnished cedar box on the back seat held his ritual paraphernalia—delicately crafted feather fans, gourd rattles with beaded
handles, eagle-bone whistle and a horsehair-tipped staff. The man
stopped the car, climbed out and began prowling through the low
shrubbery and pinon trees along the roadside.

It was close to 7 P.M. last Thanksgiving eve. Night had just fallen.
Overhead, a scrambled-egg pattern of threatening, fast-moving clouds
was illuminated by a half moon. Soon the bobbing shaft from the Navajo's flashlight held to a low bush. Returning to the car, he showed a
clump of gray-green weed in his fist. Its pungency filled the car's interior.
"Indian sage," he said, and drove onto the road again. "Good medicine,"
he added with a smile.

Two hours later, a mile from the hamlet of Sawmill, the Navajo sage
gatherer crouched on a foam-rubber pad laid at the rear of a log hogan
(the traditional, six-sided Navajo home and ceremonial house). He was
commencing his respected office as peyote "Road Chief," officiating
priest at a dusk-to-dawn session of the Native American Church, which
uses the hallucinogenic cactus, peyote, for its sacramental food. As he
began shredding the sage, a fire in the middle of the swept dirt floor was
tended by another peyote official, the "Fire Chief."

He was a stocky, elderly Navajo wearing thick glasses. His blue eyes
and impish nose betrayed his one-eighth Irish blood. Through the night's
holy hours he would often slip into the chilling outdoors to return with
armfuls of split wood, cut uniformly to ax-handle length. Now, as he
nestled new sticks into a V shape with flames crackling at the tip, the
blaze was sucked into the bare room's most prominent feature, a central
fire vent. Hanging like an overturned funnel, it narrowed into a circular
stack which shot toward the black sky through a square roof opening.

Leaning forward, the Road Chief delicately arranged a nest of sage
pods in the middle of the "altar," an earthen crescent a yard and a half
long. Known as "Peyote Moon," it curved before him like a hardened dirt
scimitar on the reddish floor. He then opened a heart-shaped, dime-store
jewelry box, and lifted out a large blossom cut from the tip of a peyote
plant, a small, hairy—but not thorny—cactus that grows profusely in the

northern Mexican desert and arid regions of south Texas. Reverently, he laid the blossom on the sage bed. This was the "Peyote Chief," symbol of the group's spiritual medium, of the "Peyote Road."

The priest swung a pointing finger along a narrow groove running the crest of the altar moon. "You follow life's road," he explained to me, "then you meet peyote, and your life changes. It has for everyone in here. We meet peyote and then we continue in that Way." Around the hogan, its side walls shrouded in thumbtacked white cloth, its ceiling a concave wheel with 23 log spokes, 15 Navajos, a Pawnee visitor and his daughter and I sat cross-legged, listening intently.

The drug which we were about to "take in" has relatively standard physiological effects, but markedly varying psychological ones, depending on the user's cultural background. Peyote's make-up of alkaloids—at least 15 at latest count, the most studied being mescaline—acts like a series of timed depth charges. First comes an unpleasant, stomach-unsettling sensation. Within a half-hour this dies, leaving a face starting to flush, pupils dilating, salivation increasing and a sense of exhilaration growing through the body, resembling the effect of swift intakes of pure oxygen. Then one moves into a period of withdrawal, of intense color awareness, of successions of hallucinations when eyes are closed, energies focused inward.

A few hours later, this levels off onto an intense plateau. Then whatever one is prompted to concentrate upon—here the cultural situation is a critical determinant—becomes uncannily luminous. During these hours, reflexes are heightened, occasional muscle twitching is common, time is overestimated, spacial perception is altered, hearing and sight yield intensified tones, ideas flow rapidly, but physical movement is awkward.

This final period, which diminishes through the following day with no aftereffects, is entered toward mid-night. Now, however, as the worshipers began the autumn Arizona night, watching their Road Chief's setting of the ritual's stage, the religious equipment was still being prepared.

"No more good cotton rope anymore," complained the Road Chief's baldish helper. He tugged at the nylon cord which was tightening a hide drumhead to an iron trade kettle. "Trouble is, it'll stretch later on," he explained, "when they start singing hard." Inside the kettle, a few soaked coals sloshed about, symbolizing fire and water to "strengthen" the drumbeats.

Then it was time for the "religious services," as the Road Chief termed them, to begin—the night's ceremonial praying and singing and confessing and weeping, which would spiral in intensity until the morning's light leaked through the door cracks 10 hours later.

Standing now, his half-red, half-navy blue peyote robe wadded regally around his waist, the Road Chief began to speak. "On this Thanksgiving, we are having this meeting to pray and sing. We made that moon there. We don't need a cathedral. High or lowly, it's all the same to Him, so it doesn't matter. We have this hogan, our Indian ways. . . ." He pointed to the dark sky which showed around the smoke hole. "We will smoke that tobacco wrapped in corn husks; we will pray to the Great Spirit, to Christ our Saviour; we are going to eat that peyote to help us. . . ."

In dozens of isolated hogans scattered through the distant mesas and canyons and high pastures of the 24,000-square-mile Navajo reservation this scene was being repeated that night. It takes place also on Christmas Eve, Easter, Armed Forces Day, the Fourth of July, at birthdays and during times of sickness or stress. Until recently the religion of the "peyote eaters" was an underground phenomenon, illegal by tribal law, the subject of fierce, though carefully hushed, controversy. Now, it is surfacing as one of the Navajos' most significant cultural crutches in a troubled time.

The largest tribe—more than 120,000 souls—among the nation's 300 Indian peoples, the Navajos seem to have entered that most painful period of their development where neither the white world nor the red world can guide their drifting cultural identities. The peyote cult, organized as the Native American Church (N.A.C.), with its unique blending of fundamentalist Christian elements and pan-Indian moral principles, seems to be meeting their deepest spiritual needs, providing relief from their shattering transitional dilemma.

Estimates of practicing Navajo membership in Arizona, New Mexico and Utah, where the "People" (the Navajo name for themselves) dwell, now run from a third to 80 per cent of the tribe. Everywhere across the reservation the ubiquitous pickup trucks bear the telltale N. A. C. decal on their rear windows, a spread-winged eagle resembling the Flexible Flyer sled insigne.

The hunger for spiritual succor arises from the mutely desperate atmosphere of the Navajo reservation. Despite recent gains in obtaining reservation industry and upgrading living standards, $700 is the average annual family income. Such facts as a life expectancy of 45 years, unemployment rates of 80 per cent in remote settlements, high infant mortality and an inordinate incidence of trachoma, pneumonia and impetigo suggest the daily reality of Navajo existence.

Between the tribe's sleek, rust-colored stone office buildings here at Window Rock, and the outlying hogans and wallboard shacks on the reservation hangs an air of palpable lostness. The desolate streets of Gallup, New Mexico, bear witness to the yawning cultural vacuum which many Navajos escape only through bouts with the bottle. An estimated 80 per cent of the tribe "has had experience with drinking problems," says a Navajo poverty worker. Probably most peyotists would agree with this figure, but for them the dark days of stumbling through Gallup's alleys were before they walked the Peyote Road. "If it keeps them from that drinking, and brings their families together again, and keeps them working, I say leave them alone," offered one crusty white storekeeper.

As much as economic depression, the erosion of traditional Navajo religion as a viable prop for community life has left the People spiritually stranded. The peyote cult is "a bridge between the old Navajo religion and Christianity," said anthropologist Editha L. Watson, seated at a long table piled with documents in the tribe's land-claims building at Window Rock. An observer of Navajo life for more than 20 years, she has attended a number of peyote meetings with her colleague, the Navajo specialist Dr. Ruth Underhill. "You see, the missionaries left the Navajos without a sense of security in their religion," Dr. Watson explained. "When they discovered peyote, it gave them a feeling of something they could hold onto."

It is hard to characterize the ancient Navajo worship without equating it with healing—physical and psychological. The varieties of "sings," multiday ceremonies run by revered medicine men, have lost their pertinency for most Navajos under 30 years of age. Despite such schemes as a recent cultural preservation project designed by the Office of Economic Opportunity to tape old songs and legends, the "Navajo Way" has dwindling ability to cure the Navajos' new insecurities. Hence, the ills which used to call a medicine man to begin a "night chant" for a distressed patient now frequently become the cause for embarkation on the Peyote Road.

The Thanksgiving peyote session near Sawmill was being "put up," as the Indians phrase it, for such a reason. The short, agitated young Navajo whose relatives were chipping in to help him sponsor the meeting had been having anxious times with his parents, who questioned peyote use. Along with this tension, dire for a family-oriented Indian, there was the problem of disposition of his grandmother's acreage, which he wished to keep intact. The meeting was to comfort the youth. Everyone's prayers would speak his name, would plead for his desires. The Road Chief ended his conversational prelude to the meeting with words to the young man: "We are having this meeting for you now. You put it up for us, and we are going to pray for you, so you'll have that understanding you want." He finished with the customary peyotist's panacea: "So you'll feel good again."

The peyote we were about to eat was the sliced and dried bud of the stubby, turnip-shaped cactus. Sometimes, the crunchy peyote "buttons," about the size of half-dollars, are eaten without further preparation, but the Navajos usually leach them of their active ingredients by boiling. Along with the resulting brown liquid, a small jar of ground-up peyote makes the rounds of the worshipers. Light green in color, the gritty, acrid powder is rolled into marble-sized balls with saliva or palm sweat as an adhesive, then chewed and swallowed.

Without this preparation, the gaseous effect of chewing peyote buttons is not unlike having a furry balloon inside your belly slowly being inflated with swamp gas. Vomiting is taken in stride, and some worshipers set tin cans beside their seating places. "My first time at a meeting," Dr. Watson recalled, "we went outside when we felt ill. When we returned to the hogan, the Fire Chief said to us: 'That was your pride coming out of you.' "

Speechlike opening prayers were droned by the Road Chief, now seated, to the accompaniment of everyone's pulling sporadically on thick corn-husk cigarettes packed with Bull Durham. A white enameled bucket of lukewarm peyote tea was passed around with a plastic cup; the container of peyote powder went with it. The meeting was fully under way. Colorful ritual gear—the fans and rattles, plume-decorated fur turbans and peyote robes the length of Mexican serapes—was brought into view, lovingly arranged. The singing began.

Although peyote did not come to the People until the nineteen-thirties, it has been a feature in Mexican Indian spirituality since before Columbus. The Spanish called the cactus the "diabolic root." The first documented consumption of the plant in the Southwest is mentioned in a 1631 Inquisition brief, describing one Francisca, a Santa Fe medicine woman, who urged a "bewitched" lady to eat peyote so she might "see" the person who had laid the spell and thus recover.

Until the last quarter of the 19th century, most data on peyote, botanically classified in 1894 as *Lophophora williamsii*, dealt with its use in what anthropologists call the "old peyote complex"—that is, it was eaten privately to induce visions or was a trance-aiding element in tribal dancing. By 1891, however, when the intrepid pioneer anthropologist James Mooney uncovered its use in Oklahoma, the "herb" had left the ceremonial sidelines to become the core of a mature "new peyote complex."

When Mooney witnessed the full-fledged "mescal rite" among the Kiowa Indians of Oklahoma, its founder, a part-Delaware, Caddo and French native of Anadarko named John Wilson, had been leading the religious movement for only a year. Wilson's nephew later gave a description of his uncle's first peyote vision which contained the primary elements that remain at the core of peyotism today:

"Peyote took pity on him and guided him into the heavenly kingdom, where, in a great vision, he saw signs and images representing events in the life of Christ. . . . He also saw the 'road' which Jesus had taken in

His ascent from the grave to the Moon in the sky and was told to remain on this road for the rest of his life, so he might be taken into the presence of Christ and of Peyote. He received precise instructions for setting up a sacred area in the peyote tent, was taught chants to be sung during the Rituals, and shown all the particulars of the ceremonial to be followed in the new cult."

His life transformed, Wilson changed his name to Big Moon and became a moralizing, proselytizing prophet, receiving hallucinatory messages and requiring his followers to abstain from liquor and avoid promiscuity. The rite diffused like wildfire through the despondent tribes crammed by various Government removals into Oklahoma. Seneca, Shawnee, Delaware, Quapaw, Potawatomi and Osage peoples took it up and bore their own peyote prophets. Variations on the ritual branched out. In 1918, peyotists from a number of tribes incorporated their movement as the Native American Church.

During the first quarter of this century, the Peyote Way spread into the Great Plains, and the Colorado Utes accepted it. These Utes were amiable neighbors of Navajos living in southern Colorado, but the People did not at first adopt the new faith. Then, in the nineteen-thirties, the Navajos experienced one of their most shattering confrontations with the white world. Without adequate emotional preparation, the Federal Government instituted a sheep reduction program among the Navajos' precious flocks to correct serious land erosion. It is not coincidence that the People, who had not joined the last-ditch redemptive movements which had swept Western Indian tribes earlier, now found comfort in peyote.

In the Four Corners region—where Colorado, Utah, Arizona and New Mexico meet—the first five Navajo Road Men were trained in the peyote mysteries. Through the thirties, the cult moved southward among the wide network of Navajo settlements. Around 1940, families in the Window Rock area started to pack the dirt from their ceremonial hogans into the shape of peyote moons. That year also began more than a quarter-century of trial for the new Navajo practitioners.

From the time of the Spanish conquest, peyote users had been described in much the pejorative terms applied to early Christians. The cactus had acquired English nicknames which indicated the general public's suspicion: "dry whisky," "white mule." Fear and ignorance of the plant's effects led many state officials, backed by most missionaries, to press successfully to make peyote use illegal by the twenties. In response, the Pueblo Indians of Taos, New Mexico, pleaded in 1922 with their white intimate, John Collier, author of the classic "Indians of the Americas," offering themselves as guinea pigs for experiments to prove the nonnarcotic, nonintoxicatory and nonorgiastic effects of eating their holy food. The National Research Council, to which Collier forwarded the idea, shelved it. (It was not until 1951 that a panel of anthropologists vindicated the Taoseños' claim, publishing a statement in *Science* that ". . . the habitual user does not develop an increased tolerance or dependence.")

In 1933 when Collier was made Indian Commissioner, he promptly "prohibited absolutely any interference by the Indian Bureau with the religious practices of the Native American Church." But state statutes and traditionalist Indian leaders were working against him. One such antipeyotist was Jacob G. Morgan, then chairman of the Navajo Tribal Council. Morgan placed the need to outlaw peyote at the top of the Tribal Council's agenda for June 3, 1940. Only one man that afternoon kept hammering at the need for more medical data. He was Hola Tso, today a venerated peyote leader, former vice president of the N. A. C. of Navajoland.

During the Thanksgiving I attended near Sawmill, Hola Tso was occupying the office of "Cedar Chief," custodian of the beaded buckskin bag containing granules of cedar sprigs which are sprinkled on the coals for sweet smoke to sanctify the prayers. Just before midnight, the Road Chief passed the prayer "pipe"—a corn-husk cigarette—to Hola Tso. From his relaxed seated position, the old man, clad in khaki shirt and jeans, gave a cadenced, long, impassioned recollection of the troubles that had begun that afternoon back in 1940.

Peyote opponents in the council chamber claimed that the hybrid cult was foreign to Navajo culture, incited gross sexual misbehavior, caused infant deformation and insanity, and posed a threat to Christianized

Navajos. The final vote was 52 to Hola Tso's lone dissent. Thereafter, the penalty for eating peyote on the reservation was nine months at hard labor or a $100 fine.

The next 27 years were hard on the peyotists, but despite its illegality, their church thrived. At 29, Albert Ross is one of the youngest Navajo council members. He was a year old when his parents began daring the punishment by holding their meetings far off the beaten track where reservation police rarely patrolled. Recently he leaned his fullback's build against a doorjamb near his Window Rock office and remembered his first peyote experience.

"I was about 8, I guess," he said. "It had been mentioned to me that this was something I should understand. I had gone to parochial school, but there was nothing there. Priests did all the praying for us. We sat in pews. In the meeting I learned that you meditate yourself, roll that tobacco yourself, you pray to God to give you strength."

Like all peyote men, Ross credits the "herb" with keeping many of his fellow Navajos from drinking. Also typically, he thanks the spiritual intercession of peyote for somehow "keeping me from having to go overseas," while asserting in the same breath: "I can defend the national flag any day." This patriotism vs. self-preservation ambivalence is common among American Indians, who are intensely chauvinistic and pragmatic at the same time. It is not that great numbers of their people have died in Vietnam, nor that they question United States policy. For Indians, death has a finiteness not assuaged by its gateway to a Christian afterlife. And it separates a man from all that makes existence worthwhile, his loved ones. Prayers for the avoidance of jeopardy with honor were frequent at the Sawmill peyote meeting.

For most of his life Ross has experienced various degrees of enforcement of the peyote ban. He and his fellow believers remember prayer sessions broken up and bags of peyote confiscated, worshipers jailed and heavy fines levied. During one interval, fired by local missionaries, vigilantes desecrated peyote altars and stole fans and robes. "It sounds like Russia, doesn't it?" Ross asks. But throughout this period membership burgeoned. "We have a lot of scars," reflects Ross. "But they taught us a lot, too."

With the peyote faction a growing force in reservation life—increasingly electing its people to the tribal council—it was just a matter of time before the 1940 law was rescinded. The first break, however, came from outside the tribe: In 1960, an Arizona state court ruled that peyote was not habit-forming and that its use was legal for N. A. C. members. In 1963, the peyotists won a moral victory with the election of a "progressive" council chairman, Raymond Nakai. Then, following his reelection in 1967, the council—after two days of heated debate—repealed its prohibition against the use or transport of peyote on the reservation.

Peyote remains a touchy subject among the Navajos. One reason, obviously, is the mysterious psychological depth of the drug experience. During the session I attended, I found it difficult to understand the antipeyotists' stated fears. The experience was surprisingly nonintoxicating. It was not myself diminished, nor a facet of my personality exaggerated, it was all of my "normal" self enlarged. Witnessing the cult's importance to those around me, however, I began to sense the concern that antipeyotists' fears were masking.

The few notations I scrawled during the height of the drug experience give only a white man's "consciousness expanded." While these then reflect an entirely different cultural context from that cloaking my companions, they may give a glimpse of peyote's power.

The rhythmic sequence of monotone prayers, shrill chanting to rapid drumming and shaking rattles, and weeping confessions had been broken with the ritual drinking of "midnight water," which comes as a refreshing break in the religious intensity. Then began the final interval until dawn.

It was sometime during this period that I managed to scrawl: ". . . the air is thick with PRESENCE . . . my eyes are windows, the glass has been taken out . . . outside me and inside, pregnant with the MYSTERY . . . want to spread beyond these hogan walls, why do we hoard the POWER. . . ."

For the Navajo, the roots to these impressions would first be filtered through a cultural set of patterns, expectations and aspirations. It is almost impossible for white people to comprehend the 24-hour-a-day spiritual life of the Indian. The peyote church falls into this rounded, unfragmented religious existence, even bringing Christianity into its old Indian mold.

It is interesting that the few whites who have seriously joined peyote ritual use have totally embraced the special Indian language and ceremony and philosophy which has grown out of the peyote cult. Its effects appear to be too unstimulating, or perhaps too psychologically profound, for today's casual "high"-seeking drug experimenters.

To the Indian, the more "medicine power"—wherever he can experience it, watch it, buy it, hear about it—the better. And the better for no-nonsense reasons. Otherwordly recompenses for living the good life have little attraction to him. Family stability, financial success, professional achievement, retention of Indian (not necessarily Navajo) identity, freedom from sickness and anxiety—these the Navajos unabashedly consider the pragmatic rewards of the Peyote Road. The People have always wanted definite results from their religion, and peyote provides them, both in the spiritual satisfaction and emotional release during the meeting's drug-intensified hours, and in the virtuous day-to-day life which peyote seems to them to foster.

The night's rounds of song and prayer seemed to circle in pitch as morning drew closer. Each in their turn, the worshipers asked the Road Chief's permission to pray and were handed the ceremonial corn-husk "smoke." As they recited the woes of reservation life, tears rolled down cheeks and soaked into worn jeans. The perils of alcohol, the break-up of a family, the loss of a child through pneumonia, the dangers of the Vietnam War—these were the threats of their in-between world. But the droning, choked prayers also thanked peyote for keeping a relative from "going overseas," for pulling an uncle off skid row, for curing a boy injured in a high-school football game, for wisdom to guide the Paris negotiators.

The taste of peyote seemed to be indelibly soaked into smoke-dried lips. The night literally "wore on." The drumming released a rainbow of tones. The PRESENCE seemed so engulfing the very air almost hummed. At some moment, alongside the fire stack, tiny snow specks fell as if in slow motion through the roof opening, hissing as they hit the metal cover. To either side of my vision the white sheeting around the walls seemed to permit peripheral vistas forever—a beckoning glowing! Then, after a seeming eternity of hours and thoughts, dawn began its own bluish glow through a cloth-covered window.

The Road Chief tootled an eagle-bone whistle, and the Pawnee girl responded, in her ceremonial role of "Peyote Woman," by carrying in the "morning water" pail. She knelt between door and fire, shyly delivering her own prayers. (For many Indian tribes, plants have gender, and Peyote Woman is at once the feminine essence of peyote, the peyote "goddess" and, according to a Taos legend, the revealer of peyote to the Indian.)

After morning water, the traditional peyote breakfast was blessed—four pans containing parched corn in sugar water; ground, boneless sweetened meat; canned fruit and candy—and handed from person to person. Each of us loaded tiny paper cups and began to eat with plastic spoons. But our circle was not broken until a final prayer by the Road Chief summed up the meeting's purpose and the hopes which had been uttered for the young host. Then the door was opened by the blood-shot-eyed Fire Chief.

Clockwise, we filed out to huddle shoulder to shoulder over a small fire, dragging deeply on ordinary cigarettes. Around us, a film of new snow covered the ground. The sky was forbiddingly gray. The men talked in whispered, confidential tones to their neighbors and one approached me. "Was it good?" he asked. "Yes," I said, and thanked him for allowing me to join them. "I prayed for you," he answered, "and for your family."

The future of peyotism is, of course, uncertain. Will it survive as a source of spiritual strength through the deep cultural revolutions certainly in store for the Navajo? Already the Navajo N. A. C. has a powerful crew of officers who protect their hard-won freedom of worship with understandable suspicion of outsiders. They are very wary of being connected in any fashion with the contemporary fascination over drug usage. Although they finally sanctioned my attendance at the Sawmill meeting, this group refused to meet collectively with me to discuss N. A. C. organization. A night-time rendezvous in a Gallup bus depot, where I was felt out by the N. A. C. vice president, did not clear me. I would have to wait.

The question of where the Peyote Road will continue, or wind up, entered the languid, comradely bantering and story-telling which customarily fill the morning hours after a meeting. Four of us were lounging around the hogan's perimeter, enjoying the lingering warmth and companionship until the noon Thanksgiving feast was laid on the floor of a shack 200 feet away. With the fire extinguished and the invasion of daylight, the interior seemed terribly bare, a different environment from that which had housed such power but hours before.

A pail had been brought inside and the earthen moon was being broken apart and carefully shoveled into it to be scattered outside. The fire's ashes, formed into an arrowhead shape by the Fire Chief, were also hauled away. The Road Chief was listening to his elderly Pawnee visitor, a man with 55 years of peyote worship behind him. Inscrutable behind sweep-around sun glasses, the old man complained that his younger Oklahoma tribesmen were practicing peyote in ways entirely new to him. The Road Chief yawned, waited politely until the old man was through, then stretched out full length, staring thoughtfully at the roof. Soon he sat up again and looked at me. "I don't know how long we will have this," he said. "I gave up my old Indian ways. I have only this way. It is good, I think.

"Maybe we won't have this in 50 years; maybe it will be gone when you come to visit my people again. But now they have this and they believe in it. You never learn all there is. Each time in here, I learn more and more.

"It is no plaything. This peyote helps you out when you call upon it, with sincerity and love inside you. We are unfortunate people, and we pray to peyote and God to have pity on us. Maybe all this will be gone some day. We don't know; but now we have it, and it is ours."

EPILOGUE:
Toward
a New Vision

Grandfathers of Our Country. Vine Deloria, Jr. | The little children stare at a picture of George of the blue eyes and white hair and seek a connection between that apparition and the statement "Father of Our Country." Seek no further, little brown-eyed, brown-skinned ones. George *is* the father of your country.

But George and Company did not spring full-blown from Hydra's head—although Indians sometimes wonder. Someone had to prepare the way for them. Someone had to help them get rid of the French. If George Washington is the father of this country because he defeated the English, then logic impels one to conclude that the men of the Iroquois are the grandfathers of this country.

George, prior to 1776, was a foreigner in America. He was an Englishman by birth and allegiance. The English, from the time they planted themselves on this shore until 1759, were waging a desperate struggle with the French for control of the North American continent. It is an established fact (at least in Indian country) that the English could not have succeeded in ousting the French if they had not had the assistance of the Iroquois Confederacy.

The league of the Iroquois was composed of six tribes: the Mohawks, the Oneidas, the Onondagas, the Cayugas, the Senecas and the Tuscarora. Actually, the Iroquois were fighting the French without the aid of

SOURCE: *New York Times*, February 22, 1972.

the British during the 1680's and the 1690's—and doing a pretty good job of it. Thus, it may be said that the Iroquois kept the French at bay until the English were strong enough to fight alongside the Confederacy.

In 1754, what is called in American history books "The French and Indian War" (conveniently ignoring the fact that the Iroquois sided with the English—George and Company) broke out. In the first major action of that war, Washington and his Virginian militiamen were forced to surrender to the Indians and their French allies. He went back for help. A year later he and his militiamen returned, accompanied by the English general Edward Braddock and 2,500 British regulars. Once again the Indians and their French allies taught the British some New World military tactics.

It wasn't until the English obtained the good offices of the Delaware Chief, Tedyuskung (whose tribes were under the protection of the Iroquois Confederacy), and a Moravian missionary, that the English were able to negotiate a peace treaty with the Indian allies of the French, and thereby secure peace on that front.

The Iroquois played an even greater role in the French and English War when the theater of action was in their own country. Alvin M. Josephy Jr., in his book, *The Indian Heritage of America*, writes: ". . . [the Iroquois] gave both direct and indirect aid to the British. Their geographical position lay athwart the principal routes connecting eastern Canada with the French positions in the Ohio Valley and Louisiana, and this fact hobbled French strategy, movements and command. At the same time, the Iroquois controlled the water routes leading from the St. Lawrence to the heart of the English colonies, and when the French tried to use them, some of the Iroquois joined the British forces in halting them. An important British victory was won at Fort William Henry, near Lake George, when a Mohawk sachem named Hendrick (of all things), responding to an appeal from his friend, Sir William Johnson, England's agent among the Iroquois, led several hundred warriors in helping the British turn back a French invasion force."

The Iroquois, being of unforked tongue, maintained their loyalty to the English long after George and Company had turned their red coats in for blue. Four of the six tribes sided with the English in the Revolutionary War. (Two remained neutral.) The colonists had to call in their old enemy, the French, and other Indian tribes to defeat the Iroquois and the English.

However, the Iroquois got their oar in when it came to laying the philosophical foundations of the new country of America. Ben Franklin noted in 1754 that, "It would be a strange thing if six capital nations of ignorant savages [???] should be capable of forming a scheme for such a union, and be able to execute it in such a manner as that it has subsisted ages and appears indissoluble; and yet that a like union should be impracticable for ten or a dozen English colonies, to whom it is more necessary and must be more advantageous, and who cannot be supposed to want an equal understanding of their interests."

Josephy writes again: "In time the structure of the league had an indirect influence not only on the union of the colonies, but on the Government of the U. S. as it was constituted in 1789. In such forms as the methods by which Congressional, Senate and House conferees work out bills in compromise sessions, for instance, one may recognize similarities to the ways in which the Iroquois league functioned."

Thus, little brown-eyed, brown-skinned ones, don't worry: One way or another Americans have an Iroquois Indian in their ancestry.

SELECTED READING

American Indian Historical Society. *The Indian Historian*, periodical magazine (1451 Masonic Avenue, San Francisco, Calif. 94117).

Bahr, Howard M; Chadwick, Bruce A.; and Day, Robert C., eds. *Native Americans Today: Sociological Perspectives*. New York: Harper & Row, 1972.

Berry, Brewton. *Almost White*. New York: Collier, 1969.

Cohen, Felix S. *Handbook of Federal Indian Law*. Albuquerque: University of New Mexico Press, 1945.

Collier, John. *From Every Zenith: A Memoir*. Denver: Alan Swallow, 1963.

de Angulo, Jaime. *Indian Tales*. New York: Hill and Wang, 1953.

Deloria, Vine, Jr. *Custer Died for Your Sins: An Indian Manifesto*. New York: Avon (W213), 1969.

Dozier, Edward P. *Hano: A Tewa Community in Arizona*. New York: Holt, Rinehart & Winston, 1966.

Fritz, Henry E. *The Movement for Indian Assimilation, 1860–1890*. Philadelphia: University of Pennsylvania Press, 1963.

Fuchs, Estelle, and Havighurst, Robert J. *To Live on This Earth: American Indian Education*. Garden City: Doubleday, 1972.

Gearing, Frederick O. *The Face of the Fox*. Chicago: Aldine, 1970.

Henry, Jeanette, ed. *The American Indian Reader: Education*. San Francisco: American Indian Historical Society, 1972.

Hertzberg, Hazel W. *The Search for an American Indian Identity: Mod-

ern Pan-Indian Movements. Syracuse: Syracuse University Press, 1971.

Leacock, Eleanor Burke, and Lurie, Nancy O., eds. *North American Indians in Historical Perspective.* New York: Random House, 1971.

Levine, Stuart, and Lurie, Nancy O., eds. *The American Indian Today.* Baltimore, Md.: Penguin Books, 1970.

McNickle, D'Arcy. *Indian Man: A Life of Oliver La Farge.* Bloomington, Ind.: University Press, 1971.

Murdock, George Peter, ed. *Ethnographic Bibliography of North America.* New Haven: Human Relations Area Files, 1960.

Murray, Keith A. *Modocs and Their War.* Norman, Okla.: University of Oklahoma Press, 1969.

Ortiz, Alfonso. *The Tewa World: Space, Time, Being and Becoming in a Pueblo Society.* Chicago: University of Chicago Press, 1969.

Prucha, Francis Paul. *American Indian Policy in the Formative Years, The Indian Trade and Intercourse Acts, 1790–1834.* Lincoln, Nebr.: University of Nebraska Press, 1970 (Bison Book BB510).

Sauer, Carl Ortwin. *Sixteenth-Century North America.* Berkeley: University of California Press, 1971.

Senungetuk, Joseph E. *Give or Take a Century: An Eskimo Chronicle.* San Francisco: American Indian Historical Society, 1971.

Sorkin, Alan L. *American Indians and Federal Aid,* Washington, D.C.: The Brookings Institution, 1971.

Spicer, Edward H. *Cycles of Conquest: The Impact of Spain, Mexico, and the United States on the Indians of the Southwest, 1533–1960.* Tucson: University of Arizona Press, 1962.

Waddell, Jack O., and Watson, O. Michael, eds. *The American Indian in Urban Society.* Boston: Little, Brown, 1971.

Walker, Deward E., Jr., ed. *The Emergent Native Americans: A Reader in Culture Contact.* Boston: Little, Brown, 1972.

Wax, Murray L.; Wax, Rosalie H.; and Dumont, Robert V., Jr. *Formal Education in an American Indian Community.* Notre Dame, Ind.: Society for the Study of Social Problems (Supplement, *Social Problems,* Volume 11, Number 4) 1964.

Wax, Murray L. *Indian Americans: Unity and Diversity.* Englewood Cliffs, N.J.: Prentice-Hall, 1971.

Wax, Rosalie H. *Doing Fieldwork: Warnings and Advice.* Chicago: University of Chicago Press, 1971.

Wilson, Edmund, *Apologies to the Iroquois.* New York: Random House, 1960 (Vintage V-313).

INDEX

A NOTE ON THE EDITORS

Murray L. Wax is Professor and Chairman of the Department of Sociology, Washington University, St. Louis, Mo. He was educated at the University of Chicago and the University of Pennsylvania. Together with Rosalie H. Wax (Professor of Anthropology, Washington University) and such American Indian associates as Robert V. Dumont, Jr., Kathryn Red Corn, and Clyde Warrior, he directed several studies of American Indian communities and the schools serving their children. He is the author of *Indian Americans: Unity and Diversity* as well as of many essays on Indian affairs and other topics.

Dr. Robert W. Buchanan is Assistant Dean of Non-Traditional Studies at Ottawa University, Ottawa, Kansas. A native of Arkansas, Dr. Buchanan holds an M.A. in history from the University of Arkansas and a Ph.D. from the American Studies Department of the University of Kansas. A specialist in Native American ethnohistory, he is preparing his dissertation "Organizational and Leadership Patterns among Contemporary Oklahoma Cherokees" for publication.